THE PRIVATE
WORLD OF
DAPHNE DU
MAURIER

THE PRIVATE WORLD OF DAPHNE DU MAURIER

Martyn Shallcross

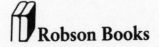

Robson Books

First published in Great Britain in 1991 by
Robson Books Ltd, Bolsover House,
5–6 Clipstone Street, London W1P 7EB

Copyright © 1991 Martyn Shallcross

The right of Martyn Shallcross to be identified
as author of this work has been asserted by him in
accordance with the Copyright, Designs and Patents Act 1988

British Library Cataloguing in Publication Data

Shallcross, Martyn
The private world of Daphne du Maurier.
1. Du Maurier, Daphne, 1907–1989
I. Title
823.912

ISBN 0 86051 669 5

Photoset in North Wales by
Derek Doyle & Associates, Mold, Clwyd.
Printed in Great Britain by
Butler & Tanner Ltd., Frome and London

For Bernice, who first introduced me
to the private world of Daphne du Maurier, with love.

'As long as memories last, love will never die.'

Contents

Contents

Acknowledgements

First of all I should like to thank the late Dame Daphne du Maurier for her help over the years with the writings I have attempted concerning her career. Thanks also to her son, Christian Browning. My sincere thanks, once again, to Joan Fontaine for her help and support at all times, to my agent, Anne Dewe, and to Susan Rea.

Also, thanks to Sir Alec and Lady Merula Guinness, Sir Douglas Fairbanks Jnr, Sir Rex Harrison, Sir John Gielgud and Nicolas Roeg for allowing me moments of their time during their hectic schedules.

In New York, London and Hollywood I should like to thank the following: Alan Bates, the late Ingrid Bergman, Muriel Box, Faith Brook, Sally Burton, Julie Christie, Nigel Davenport, Joanna David, Michael Dennison, Lady Fitzwilliam, Bryan Forbes, Edward Fox, Major-General John Frost and the Airborne Museum, Aldershot; Michael Gough, Stewart Granger, Dulcie Grey, Susan Hampshire, Valerie Hobson, Deborah Kerr, Jesse Lasky Jnr, Sophia Loren,

Hilary Mason, Nova Mather, Sarah Miles, Sir John Mills, Roy Moseley, Pete Murray, Nanette Newman, Maureen O'Hara, Tamsin Olivier, Jack Profumo, Jane Seymour, Pat Silver, Donald Sutherland, Nora Swinburne, Elizabeth Taylor, Sir Peter Ustinov, and Brook Williams. A special thanks to Victor Spinetti for encouraging me to write about Daphne in the first place.

In Cornwall I should like to thank Cyril and Rosemary Blackstock, David Clarke, Isabelle Dunn, Tommy Dunn, Mary and Pam Fox, Gladys Hooper and her stepsister Violet Lemin, Val and David Jones, June Lander, Esther Rowe, Dr A L Rowse, Michael Williams, Colin Wilson, BBC Radio Cornwall and all those who do not wish any mention.

In Staffordshire, Pat Cuxson, Barbara Mart, Jackie May, Hilary Minster, Alison O'Brien and Anthony Smith, and, at the Alexandra Theatre, Birmingham, Alistair Corrigan and Paul Greenfield.

Foreword

Making the film of Daphne du Maurier's *Rebecca* with Alfred Hitchcock, in 1940, was a learning time. He combined two attributes of a great cinema director – he knew acting, and he knew visual mood. He would sketch on a large drawing pad exactly the effects that he wanted.

One such drawing was of 'I' de Winter, the character I played, cringing in an oversized wing chair, light just across her face, so that only the terrified eyes peered out. The rest was in darkness. We could all see precisely what he wished to photograph. Hitchcock had taste, he had imagination. His technique was 'Divide and Conquer'. He wanted total loyalty, but only to him.

I enjoyed meeting Daphne du Maurier in 1978 at her beautiful home, Kilmarth, and visiting her private world – and the locations for so many of her books – during my Cornish vacation. Somehow, I feel that Daphne's spirit has not left Cornwall and, when I awaken each morning to see her photo on my dressing-table, I know she has formed part of me through her writings and her friendship.

I owe her a great deal, for in the story of Rebecca we both shared the same dream. For that I shall be eternally grateful.

1

Discovering Daphne

> 'Little notes, scrawled on half-sheets of paper, and letters... Her voice, echoing through the house, and down the garden, careless and familiar like the writing in the book.'
> *Rebecca*

It looked as though I wouldn't even be able to go for a walk that day. Outdoor exercise was completely out of the question. My family spent many holidays in Cornwall, sometimes near Fowey and sometimes west of Penzance – in fact my mother told me that she had taken her very first steps on Marazion beach, just opposite St Michael's Mount. Now I was about four, and she and I were staying on the
x south-east coast of Cornwall, just outside the pretty town of Looe. Then, unexpectedly – on that day towards the end of July 1958 – the late-morning sun began to send occasional gleams through rifts in the heavy clouds. My mother looked at the sky again, and decided we would go on a boating expedition.

X: N.E. SURELY — NO, THE AUTHOR IS RIGHT!

1

Not shark-fishing, I hoped desperately. All that blood and guts made me feel quite sick. But no, my mother wasn't much keener on it than I was. Her idea was that we would go and visit a famous house; one, she told me, immortalized in a film and a novel. My spirits soared as I heard that the lady who had written the story actually lived there. And when our boat sailed out of Looe harbour the sun finally broke through. We were in search of Daphne du Maurier's Manderley, that mysterious house of secrets.

This make-believe mansion seemed to have captured so much of my mother's imagination that she paid little attention to the coast, or to the other places of interest we passed. One piece of coastline can look just like another – but the Cornish coast with its rugged rocks stretching upward to dark brown cliffs, with the sea crashing underneath, made me think of danger and adventures and excitement.

Our cruise carried on and on until eventually the full extent of Fowey harbour was stretched out in front of us. To the left lay the old town of Fowey, with brightly painted cottages and a skyline dominated by its beautiful church and clock tower, while to the right the clustered cottages of Polruan were scattered across the headland to reach the picturesque harbour clinging to the edge of the village. I had never seen anything so compelling and mystifying, and the image of this place we had suddenly arrived at remains with me still.

Around the harbour of Fowey we sailed, and finally out again. We passed the old castle and rounded Gribbin Head to Polridmouth Bay. I could see a pebble and sand beach, a stone cottage at the edge of a piece of water, and behind that dense trees and shrubs. I turned to my mother. 'Where's Manderley? Is it a real house?'

'Be patient,' my mother replied. 'It's surrounded by woods. The lady who lives there is a recluse – that means she doesn't want to be seen.' We beached our craft, found a suitable place to spread a rug and laid out the picnic. Only the sound of the sea and the gulls high above us disturbed the peace and tranquillity.

As we ate our late lunch I noticed that we were not alone. A small figure, a solitary-looking person, appeared as if by magic or conjured up from the spirit world. She seemed a fairy thing, no one real at all. As the figure approached I could make out that it was a lady, her grey hair almost covered by a cap pulled down to obscure her face. Trailing behind her followed a small dog, no longer young, and an array of cats.

'Good afternoon.' The lady spoke first.

'Hello. Is it true you write books?' I enquired with a child's curiosity.

'Of course,' was the quick and firm answer. 'Can you read yet?'

'I think so,' I replied confidently.

After a few more pleasantries the lady departed, leaving me with the memory of her blue, almost impish, eyes.

'She's not someone who doesn't want to be seen,' I thought. I had liked this famous writer, and I hoped we would meet again.

It is interesting to look back and try and work out why a certain author, book or film stays in one's mind for a lifetime. Perhaps there are many reasons. Like many children, during adolescence I was fascinated by films and movie stars. I was particularly keen on the classic films produced by Hollywood in the 1940s, films such as *Mrs Miniver*, *Random Harvest* and *Rebecca* – all filmed in the

United States, though using English casts. The England they portray is distant and dreamlike, represented as it should have been and not as it was. Escapist they may have been, but very stylish and polished.

Not many years after my first meeting with Daphne du Maurier I was living with my Aunt Bernice (a trained singer, who had sung in oratorios all over the country) and my grandparents at their home in the centre of the pretty historic north Staffordshire village of Abbots Bromley (famous world-wide for its extraordinary and unique Horn Dance). Norfolk House is Tudor in origin, and felt extremely large to the child I still was. One afternoon in the early 1960s I was left alone to watch television in the large front drawing-room. The film I was engrossed in was Alfred Hitchcock's version of *Rebecca*, shown for the umpteenth time. As I watched the story unfold on the screen, I remembered that visit to Cornwall and wondered about the house, Manderley – was it real or not? The conclusion of the film, as everyone who has watched it will remember, shows the destruction of Manderley in an all-consuming fire.

Shortly after the film had finished, Grandmother and Aunt Bernice decided we should go out in the car – and as we reached the roadway a fire engine sped past, siren blaring. Out of curiosity we followed and eventually, after careering along many narrow lanes, the fire engine stopped at the back of Blithfield Hall. The large rectory behind it, a three-storey building looking not unlike the fictitious Manderley, was on fire. As we watched the house burn we saw floors give way, ceilings collapse, furniture fall into the burning embers, and finally – in a moment of supreme drama – the roof caved in. This remarkable scene was to stay locked in my mind for many years and eventually it would lead to a friendship with Daphne du Maurier.

I next became aware of her existence when I was at prep school, a former stately home set in extensive grounds, complete with a lake and woods. I was fascinated by large houses, and someone gave me an article to read about Menabilly, the Cornish home Daphne du Maurier had lived in for many years. I looked at this beautiful and angular house, set among acres of Cornish woods, and felt I must get to know it better.

My grandmother, my mother and my aunt had all read her novels, and were intrigued particularly by the story of *Rebecca*. When my mother had remarried, and was expecting a baby, she announced that, if she had a daughter, she would call her Rebecca. (However, a close friend had a daughter first and named her child Rebecca.) The impact of Daphne du Maurier's novels left a lasting impression on me through their impression on other members of my family.

However, despite all those childhood holidays in Cornwall (apart from that one brief meeting when I was a very small child), I had not met Daphne. She was known to be unsociable and, as my mother had said, a recluse – someone very few people knew or saw. Like most of her readers, I believed she spent her life in isolation in Cornwall.

It was entirely by chance that I finally met her in the late 1960s, and then it was not in her beloved Cornwall but on Crete, still a largely unspoilt island. This meeting was completely unexpected – the last person I had expected to meet on holiday was one of our most famous writers.

My beloved grandmother, and then my grandfather, had died; my mother had a new home and family, and I lived with Aunt Bernice. We had gone on holiday to Crete, to the then small and picturesque fishing village of Ayios Nikólaos; we were staying at the beautiful Minos Beach Hotel, set in semi-tropical gardens which stretched down to the edge of the Gulf of Merabéllou. After dinner in the hotel, I walked around the reception area where I noticed a small lady, wearing trousers. She was examining some postcards.

'Hello,' she said casually, still looking at the cards.

'Hi,' was my rather limited start to a conversation. 'Beautiful weather, isn't it?'

'I hope so,' the unknown lady answered, sounding optimistic.

Before long our conversation became more involved, and each time we met – sometimes in the morning, but more often after dinner – we talked a little more. Soon Aunt Bernice and I found ourselves on first-name terms, as one often does with people met on holiday, with Daphne du Maurier, her son, Christian (known as Kits), and his beautiful Irish wife.

'Would you like to accompany us to Spinalonga?' Daphne's kind invitation included us both, so Aunt Bernice and I joined her on the excursion. We took a rather rustic motor-boat from the harbour, and went along the coast to the island of Spinalonga – a former leper colony. Daphne enjoyed the voyage, and as we walked round the island, examining the ruined buildings, she showed her fascination with these decayed properties and the lives of the former occupants. Did she perhaps feel there was a story there that she might write, I wondered.

Daphne became more expansive, and talked more, during the last few days of our holiday; and I found that we had a lot in common, particularly our tastes in literature and music. Unfortunately, before we could really spend time together, our holiday drew to its end – unexpected, as the ends of all holidays are. And, as always, promises were made to keep in touch.

It was during this brief holiday friendship that I became

aware of Daphne's sense of humour. She was not a stuffy person, or unprepared to have fun. Her modern attitude to life was one of the reasons that she was able to bridge the generation gap.

She had given me an open invitation to visit her at any time, and on my return home I intended to write. Alas, other matters got in my way and months passed by. Like many teenagers, I was preoccupied with my own affairs and the need for starting some sort of career. I intended to work for a while before going on to further education, and I was accepted by the Civil Service. I had hoped to join the Diplomatic Corps, but this did not turn out as planned, and with some trepidation I accepted a job in the Cabinet Office.

London and Whitehall seemed a big leap from Staffordshire and holidays in Cornwall, but before I took up my post Aunt Bernice and I were able to spend an enjoyable fortnight in the Cornish village of Mousehole. At the end of it we decided to break our long journey home with a night or so in Fowey – and while we were there we would take up Daphne's invitation.

As we made our way to where we thought she lived, we discovered that visitors were not encouraged. Her home was well hidden and it took us a while to find the gateway, for there was no sign outside the entrance; it was not until we had advanced quite some way along the drive (made famous in her novel, *The House on the Strand*) that we saw just how large and impressive the house she rented was. Typically Cornish in construction, and built as the dower house to Menabilly, where Daphne had lived from 1943 to 1969,the front of Kilmarth that faced us as we approached was – like that of many old houses thereabouts – part slate and part stone. Aunt Bernice and I conferred briefly, and decided on the back door.

Would Daphne remember me? I felt nervous as I rang the doorbell. A tall lady with black hair, whom I judged from her looks to be Cornish, came to the door. (I learned later that this was Esther Rowe, secretary and housekeeper to Daphne for many years.) She greeted me with a smile, and I asked what must have been a question she heard often: 'Is this where Daphne du Maurier lives?'

'Yes,' came the rather quick and sharp reply, 'but I am afraid she will not see you. I expect she will sign your books.' She had spotted the copies of *The House on the Strand* and *My Cousin Rachel* we were holding, and we stood there by the back door until Esther Rowe returned. 'I am sorry,' she said, 'I am afraid she is out. Can you call back later?'

'No, it's all right,' I told her, disheartened by what I felt was an unfriendly response. 'I'm sure she won't remember me anyway.'

Aunt Bernice and I returned to the car. Rather hesitantly, I suggested waiting to see if Daphne walked down the drive. Our patience was rewarded — after several long minutes, there was Daphne, her dog at her heels. She was coming from the direction of the house, and she walked quickly, with her cap pulled over her head; she had not seen us at all.

'Excuse me,' I shouted, 'may we have a word with you?'

Daphne turned round, looking surprised. 'Of course.'

As she signed my books I reminded her of our meeting in Crete, and she seemed to remember. As often happens in Cornwall, the rain had suddenly begun to fall without warning.

'Let's go into the garage for shelter,' said Daphne. So the three of us entered the rather dilapidated building, and we talked further. I was not the only one on whom Crete had made a tremendous impression. In fact, Daphne told us, she had written a short story based on the holiday we had shared with her. (It was included in the collection of stories called *Not After Midnight*, and the title story became famous as the film *Don't Look Now*.)

'Are you writing anything at the moment?' I asked.

Her reply was quick and to the point. 'I have just finished a novel, called *Rule Britannia*. It has nearly killed me.' Now that I could see her close to, the first thing I noticed was that she looked older, and seemed smaller, than I remembered. Her face was lightly powdered, and her tiny features looked lined and pinched. Somehow her whole appearance gave the impression that she was a tourist who had overstayed her welcome. She was eccentric, I realized; there was no doubt about that. Finally we said goodbye and Daphne walked off towards her home, the little dog trotting behind. She raised her hand in the air in a final gesture of farewell.

I returned home to the beginnings of the career I'd worried about. I had left school and now I started my new job in Whitehall, in the Cabinet Office. Working in Lord Rothschild's department, the so-called 'Think Tank', was very interesting – but government service and I were unsuited to each other. After only a few weeks I returned home to Aunt Bernice. She encouraged me to further my education, and I enrolled at the West Midlands College in Walsall with the idea that I would eventually become a teacher. While I was there, events occurred which furthered my friendship with Daphne. I became very friendly with the writer, Jesse Lasky Jr, and his wife, Pat. Jesse has written several novels, volumes of poetry and plays as well as many screenplays, and at this time he and Pat were working on a book on the lives of Vivien Leigh and Laurence Olivier. It was eventually published as *Love Scene*, and they asked if I would help with the research. My career had taken yet another direction: this turned out to be the beginning of my connection with show business.

As part of my research, I had to write to Daphne, asking for her help with details of the Hitchcock film of *Rebecca*, which had starred Laurence Olivier as Maxim de Winter and Joan Fontaine as his unnamed second wife. Daphne and I began to correspond regularly over a variety of topics. At first her letters were short and precise, later they became more familiar, and indeed longer. As the work on the book progressed, Daphne became intrigued, remembering that, years ago – when she was a young and inexperienced girl and he a very young man – Jesse had visited the du Maurier family home in Hampstead, Cannon Hall.

Whenever I mentioned the idea of visiting Fowey, and calling at Kilmarth to see her, Daphne always wrote back, 'I don't think it's the right moment for Cornwall.' Eventually, after several months of correspondence, an invitation was forthcoming, and after several more long letters a lunch date was arranged. Daphne added one condition to the invitation, and that was that after lunch I should help her exercise her dogs in the fields, and keep the cows away from them.

Aunt Bernice and I made the long and tiring journey down to Cornwall, and we arrived at Fowey in the evening. The view from the Fowey Hotel was breathtaking as always, and the vista of Polruan across the harbour would have held me spellbound if I hadn't been conscious that I must let Daphne know I'd arrived. I rang her from my hotel room.

'I thought you were coming to lunch today. What happened?' she demanded.

Lost for words, I tried to placate her.

'Well, then, you won't be able to have roast chicken. You will have to make do with chicken fricassee!'

The next day Aunt Bernice dropped me at the end of the

drive to Kilmarth, and I walked its length to the imposing front door. Daphne greeted me warmly and led me into what she called the 'long drawing-room' – it is, in fact, more than forty feet long – installed me in a chair opposite her and offered me a small glass of Dubonnet. She did not remember having met me, either in Crete or in her garage (no one could expect her to have remembered the brief meeting on the beach so many years ago), but told me, 'I usually forget names, then remember faces.'

Lunch was served by Esther Rowe, whom I'd first seen at Kilmarth's back door. 'I am afraid there is no wine,' Daphne said, 'but you can have some lager my son left behind. You will have to help yourself to the food, I live very simply now.'

During our meal the telephone rang several times, and Daphne went into the hall to take the calls. On one occasion I heard her say, 'I don't do personal appearances.' Apparently it was a request to open a fête that she had so quickly dealt with. 'Why can't they get the vicar's wife, or someone else, to open the fête?' she asked me. 'What do they want me for?'

When she wanted to know what my ambitions were, I explained that I should like to write for a living. Daphne told me that when she had started writing, she had never found it difficult to get her work published.

I knew that her grandfather, George du Maurier, had been an eminent artist and illustrator, a caricaturist whose illustrations for *Punch* were acute commentaries on the Victorian scene. He also wrote three successful novels, of which the best-known nowadays is *Trilby* – the story of an artist's model who falls under the spell of the musician, Svengali; he trains her voice and she becomes a famous singer, but his influence over her was such that when he dies her voice collapses, she loses her eminence and finally dies also. George's younger son, Gerald, Daphne's father, gave up a business career for the stage; he became a successful and very popular actor manager, and was knighted in 1922 for his services to the stage. Daphne had written a memoir of her father, *Gerald: A Portrait*, in 1934 (the year of his death) and in 1951 she edited a selection of the letters of her grandfather. Her family connections, of which she was proud and conscious, had undoubtedly helped her career. Daphne's advice to me was to work on a newspaper, and then progress into writing books from there.

After lunch, she showed me around her treasured home. First we went upstairs into what she called her 'suite'; this consisted of a bedroom, a dressing-room and an *en-suite* bathroom. I noticed on the walls several cartoons of the notorious Mary Anne Clarke, her great-great-grandmother – she was the mistress of Frederick, Duke of York from about 1803 to 1807, and the cartoons showed her in bed with her lumpy royal lover. Daphne's sense of humour had led her to hang these satirical comments on past scandals in her bedroom.

Later, we went downstairs. She showed me a large room at one end of Kilmarth in which a wide picture window looked out over the fields towards the sea and Frenchman's Creek. I could imagine the waiting ship and Dona St Columb stealing across the fields to her handsome lover ...

All the rooms were filled with an enormous amount of clutter: books, postcards, dried flowers, photographs of royalty and family portraits of her three children (Tessa, whose marriage, to the son of the war hero, brought her the title of Countess Montgomery of Alamein, Flavia, whose second marriage made her Lady Leng, and Kits) and of herself when young. Daphne was like a jackdaw, and had put all these items together without any thought as to how they looked.

Pride of place, however, was given to the medals which had belonged to her husband, Lieutenant-General Sir Frederick ('Tommy') Browning. These were prominently displayed in the dining room, where they could not be overlooked. Daphne had, in some respects, hero-worshipped her handsome husband; she had admired him in much the same way that she had admired her father.

In the basement of Kilmarth, she showed me the fourteenth-century foundations that had interested her so much. In one corner she had created a chapel or shrine with items such as more of her husband's medals and his dress sword, as well as some semi-precious stones that seemed to have a great importance for her.

After showing me the house, Daphne pulled on her Wellington boots, a thick jacket and her cap. Outside, while her two white West Highland terriers trailed behind us, we walked away from Kilmarth across the fields, with the view of St Austell and Frenchman's Creek in the background.

It was during this walk, and subsequent walks like it, that Daphne told me so much about her private world. 'Everything I have written, you know, happened within an arm's length of this house, and Menabilly of course.' As we progressed down to the seashore, she pointed out the distant buildings of the farm, Menabilly Barton, and told me how she had got her idea for the story of 'The Birds' when she was out walking one day. She had glanced across the fields to where Tommy Dunn was ploughing, and seen the birds flocking down to the newly turned soil behind his tractor.

On our return to Kilmarth, I realized that my visit was coming to an end and the time was approaching for me to return to the Fowey Hotel. 'I'll drive you back,' Daphne offered. We got into her car and proceeded down the road on our way back to Fowey. As we approached the crossroads at Four Turnings, just outside the town, she turned to me. 'I described these crossroads at the beginning and end of my novel, *My Cousin Rachel*. They used to hang people here many years ago, you know.'

Daphne also pointed out the old carriage drive to her former home, Menabilly. The driveway was overgrown and the gate chained and padlocked. 'This is the drive that I describe in Rebecca, at the beginning of the novel. You know, the words that people seem to like so much: "Last night I dreamt I went to Manderley again ...".'

Parking is always difficult in the busy little town of Fowey, so Daphne pulled up on double yellow lines. Before leaving the car, I thanked her for the pleasant lunch and placed a large kiss on her powdered cheek. With great surprise, she declared, 'Well, I have enjoyed meeting you!'

'Do come and say hello to my aunt,' I suggested.

'I thought you were alone. You never told me you had an aunt!' She walked back with me into the Fowey Hotel, where she exchanged pleasantries with Aunt Bernice, then smiled and said her farewells rather quickly. We watched from the hotel as Daphne reversed her small car the wrong way up a one-way street, shouting through the window as she did so, 'Oh, it's all right! They won't say anything. I've lived here for years, you know!'

I phoned Daphne before we left to return to our Staffordshire home, and was delighted when she said, 'Write to me when you get home, and we will talk further.'

After that, I spoke to Daphne at least once a fortnight, and time and distance did not stop our further meetings, although we lived hundreds of miles away from each other. Throughout the 1970s our meetings took place mainly at holiday times, for we continued to take holidays in Cornwall and I always tried to visit her. The book on Laurence Olivier and Vivien Leigh progressed, and news of it would remind Daphne of long-ago events. She recalled one meeting with Olivier and Leigh: 'I remember having dinner at Douglas Fairbanks Jnr's, and I sat next to Olivier. He talked charmingly about my father, Gerald, which greatly pleased me.' Her memory of the past could sometimes seem clouded, but at other times it was clear and precise. The further back her thoughts went, the more she remembered. She often said, 'My childhood in London and Cornwall I think was interesting, but I feel I was boring after my marriage.'

It was during this period that Daphne let me know how she felt about reactions to her work. 'You know the public see me essentially as a novelist, and not as a serious writer like a biographer.' She made this comment after reading adverse critical reaction to her book *The Winding Stair*, based on the lives of the brothers, Anthony and Francis Bacon. (Anthony, the elder, was a diplomatist, while Francis was Lord Chancellor from 1618 to 1621 and is credited by some people with Shakespeare's works.) Daphne found writing a difficult process, and the failure of critics over the years to take her seriously greatly upset her.

Colin Wilson, the well-known writer on the occult, remembered a visit to Daphne when she was still living at Menabilly. 'I was always a great admirer of Daphne's, and I realize that she was often hurt by the fact that the "highbrow" critics never took her seriously. Long before I met her, at about the time I was coming to live in Cornwall, I talked to Hilary Rubinstein at Gollancz's about her. He told me he had been talking to a man about her work, just as she was about to bring out a volume of stories – I think it was

The Apple Tree – and the man said, "Oh, I expect it is sure to be bad." Hilary asked, "Why, have you read some of her previous stories?" The man said, "No, but she sells so many copies that she is bound to be bad." I know this kind of reaction hurt Daphne very much, and I felt that a lot of the time she was very unsure of herself.'

As my friendship with Daphne developed through our letters, I began to understand her personality more. And, whenever we met, Daphne seemed unable to stop talking, which proved to me that she was indeed lonely. Daphne's children had been married for many years, and had left home at an early age. None of them lived near her, and so she only saw them occasionally – usually around holiday times.

It was knowing of my fascination with films and movie stars that led Daphne to tell me about the stars associated with the film adaptations of her novels. This culminated in a letter she sent me in May 1978: 'Do come to Cornwall in August. Joan Fontaine has asked to meet you, come along and I will introduce you.' This was wonderful news: at that time I was planning a film tribute to Joan Fontaine, to be given in the auditorium of the National Film Theatre (it seats more than four hundred people) in London. Aunt Bernice and I arranged another Cornish holiday for August: we would stay first of all to the west of Penzance, and then have ten days in Fowey.

The weather was exceptionally good in early August 1978, and it was with some reluctance that we left our small hotel just outside Penzance. When we arrived at the Fowey Hotel, I rang Daphne to let her know we were there and to get any news of Joan Fontaine's whereabouts. Sounding very surprised, Daphne said, 'Oh dear! She came for lunch yesterday. I have told her about you, and your proposed film tribute.'

I felt disappointed, and Daphne must have gauged some of this from our conversation. 'Bring your aunt tomorrow,' she said, 'at about twelve o'clock, and we will have a pleasant lunch and talk further.'

Daphne was at her front door to greet us, and embraced me as I entered Kilmarth. Over lunch she told us of her meeting with Joan, and how good the actress looked. Daphne was also intrigued because Joan's sister, Olivia de Havilland, had never got along with Joan. Upon hearing this information, Aunt Bernice told Daphne how difficult her own family were, and how my mother had gradually ceased all communication. 'I know some families do fall out,' Daphne told us, 'but my sisters, Angela and Jeanne, are like that.' And she lifted her hands in the air, in a gesture of closeness.

This was the first time Aunt Bernice had been inside Kilmarth, and Daphne proudly took her on a guided tour of the house and grounds. She showed us all the original manuscripts of her celebrated novels, including that of *Rebecca*. I recall that parts of it were written in longhand. Daphne's son, Kits, whom we'd met on Crete, was staying at Kilmarth with his family, and he was happy to play photographer with my camera – for the guided tour had been got through quickly enough to leave time for taking pictures.

When we returned to the hotel I found that I must have left a few things (among them the lens cover for my camera) in the long drawing-room. But the next day, as Aunt Bernice and I drank our morning coffee, Daphne arrived. She was dressed in a blue tracksuit, with her usual cap pulled down over her head. She tiptoed through the hotel, hoping that no one would recognize her. Again, she greeted me warmly; we embraced, and she handed me the things I had left behind.

'Would you like coffee?' I asked her.

'Of course,' she replied. 'Let's sit on the balcony. We can watch the view of Polruan and the harbour.' As we sat with our coffee, enjoying the view and chatting amiably, I noticed that people in the bar were intrigued to see their famous novelist out and about. The cap had not prevented them from recognizing Daphne du Maurier.

Daphne decided to change her mind once again. 'Let's have a drink. Some Dubonnet would be fun!' Our drinks arrived, and as we enjoyed them Daphne began to recall moments from the past. 'You see that cross at the entrance to the harbour? Years ago, Angela and I used to go nude swimming there.' She also talked about the village of Polruan, and we learned that the view before us had encouraged her to write her first novel, *The Loving Spirit*.

During our conversation, Daphne told me that Joan Fontaine would allow me to interview her in London in the autumn, when she returned to publicize her autobiography, *No Bed of Roses*. Once more, Daphne described this idea as 'fun', and even suggested that she herself might attend the public interview at the National Film Theatre.

After our return home to Staffordshire, Daphne rang or wrote several times a week during the next few months to see how things were progressing. A date in November was set for my interview with Joan, and when the day arrived the Controller of the National Film Theatre hosted a lunch at the Connaught Hotel. Joan was there, of course, and my other guests were Jesse Lasky Jr and Pat, Aunt Bernice and another friend. Joan was very nervous throughout lunch, and she told me she would prefer all the film clips illustrating her career to be shown first, and then to be followed by the discussion. Daphne and her family did not attend and so missed seeing Joan give a stunning performance. After it the audience rose to their feet, giving her a standing ovation. Roy

Moseley, the biographer of Cary Grant, said afterwards that he thought Joan's performance was second only to that of Bette Davis for entertainment value.

My career had progressed to include interviewing for the BBC, and Daphne took a keen and warm interest in what I did. When I went to Cornwall I always took with me photographs of stars or directors I had recently met, and Daphne enjoyed seeing them and hearing my stories. Though her own family seemed to have no interest in show business, she liked to hear all the latest gossip. I remember she was most concerned when I told her of Ingrid Bergman's illness: she had developed cancer of the breast in 1973, and fought bravely against it until her death in 1982.

On one occasion I went down to Cornwall in early October, accompanied as ever by Aunt Bernice; we also had with us a friend from Lichfield, who was recovering from a car accident. When I rang, Daphne asked me, 'What do the girls like to drink?' 'Sherry will be fine,' I told her, knowing how she worried that people would be upset if the wrong drinks were presented.

Margaret, our friend from Lichfield, was overawed by Daphne's large house and its grounds. She sat spellbound in the long drawing-room of Kilmarth as Daphne told her how she had written *Rebecca*. Most people found meeting Daphne rather intimidating, but she was always pleasant and on this occasion she signed copies of *Vanishing Cornwall* for Margaret and for Aunt Bernice. Daphne considered people's names with interest; as she signed my aunt's copy, she said, 'Yes, Bernice would be a good name for a character in one of my novels.'

Daphne became more difficult to see towards the end of her life, preferring her own company and rejecting requests to go out. For many years she had hated eating in public, except abroad. 'That's different, isn't it?' she would state. Until 1981 she enjoyed reasonably good health. Each day she would go out and walk, with her dogs, for she believed the fresh air made her feel well. Her love for the Cornish coastline never faded or grew cold, and it was a love affair that would last till her death.

After publication of *The Rebecca Notebook* in 1981, Daphne started to feel unwell. During the autumn she visited Scotland with the hope of finding some ideas for a forthcoming novel, but her imagination had deserted her: age was catching up with one of the greatest story-tellers of the twentieth century. Her career had come full circle. I tried to interest her in restarting it, but my attempts always failed. The ideas had finally stopped.

I had discovered Daphne, and through the years I knew her she allowed me time, she gave me something of herself, that I would never forget. Despite her fame she could seem insecure and unprepared for the attention someone in her position inevitably receives, attention which other people too could find disconcerting. Fame creates its own barriers: I recall a day when friends of mine, a teacher and her daughter, went with me to Kilmarth. As we arrived Daphne too drew up in her car, accompanied by her nurse-companion and – as ever – two little dogs.

Daphne got out of her car, seeming pleased to see me, and placed a large kiss on my cheek. I carried one of her dogs into the house and we both went into the long drawing-room, leaving my two friends in the car. After a short while Esther Rowe called down to them, saying, 'Would you like a cup of coffee with Lady Browning?'

'No, thank you,' replied my two friends in unison, and put up their papers and pretended to read them. The affection

A debonair photograph of Gerald du Maurier appearing in *Arsène Lupin*.

A young Daphne around the publication of *The Loving Spirit* in 1931. (*Popperfoto*)

The du Maurier holiday home in Fowey Harbour was a Swiss-type cottage called Ferryside. The figurehead seen to the right is from the *Jane Slade*, the wreck that gave Daphne the idea for her first n

The original pub sign (*above left*) stood for many years outside the wayside inn made famous in Daphne's novel *Jamaica Inn*. On seeing Alfred Hitchcock's film adaptation of the book, which starred Maureen O'Hara and Charles Laughton, Daphne was not pleased, as it differed widely from the original. However, after the success of the film of *Rebecca, Jamaica Inn* was re-released.

Alfred Hitchcock's Piece de Resistance in Screen Thrillers

PATHE PRESENTS THE RE-RELEASE OF

JAMAICA IN

starring CHARLES LAUGHTON; MAUREEN O'HARA
ROBERT NEWTON, EMLYN WILLIAMS, LESLIE BANKS

From the sensational novel by Daphne du Maurier
of which over one million copies have been sold.

Directed by ALFRED HITCHCOCK

Daphne showed me had surprised them, and in many ways they were almost jealous that I knew such a well known and celebrated person.

Daphne could show another side to her personality. I rang to wish her a happy birthday in 1982, and our conversation ended with her saying, 'I must go, dear, there are some people coming down the drive with their books. I shall have to go and sign them. Bless you, dear.' At that stage she still enjoyed the attention her readers gave her, and she still quite liked these meetings.

Although Daphne had stated on many occasions that she didn't want anyone to write about her in her lifetime, she had encouraged me to write about the settings of some of her most famous Cornish books. This was the countryside which, over the years, had provided her with the background to all her greatest successes: *The Loving Spirit*, *Jamaica Inn*, *Rebecca*, *Frenchman's Creek*, *The King's General*, *My Cousin Rachel* and *The House on the Strand* were all set in Cornwall, and many towns and historic beauty spots have been immortalized by Daphne's descriptive narratives. But how many people, I wondered, knew the true locations of the exciting stories they read? The private world of Daphne du Maurier had remained secret for many years, and the door had always been locked to outsiders. The names and places that inspired her are as beautiful as what she wrote about them. When my *Daphne du Maurier Country* was published in 1987, two years before her death, Daphne inscribed a copy for me: 'For Martyn. You are the only person who can really write about me.'

It is quite easy to see why certain places inspired Daphne to weave tales of suspense and drama around them. She was an artist who painted her pictures with words; and her style of narrative writing could conjure up rich dramatic scenes as she combined fact with fiction in the setting of a real place. For more than half a century she entertained us with pictures of life drawn from her imagination. Like the famous Brontë sisters, Daphne lived through the characters she created.

Although by the time of her death Daphne was a recluse, her life had been anything but uneventful. People all over the world admired her work, though much about her remained unknown to them. Throughout her life she had mixed with celebrities from the world of the theatre, and with the royal family. She knew Her Majesty the Queen, Prince Philip, Gertrude Lawrence and Gladys Cooper. Daphne was unique among writers because she was able to combine her writing and the fame it brought her with friendships with royalty. Her marriage to Frederick Browning, whose eventual career was as a member of the royal household, took Daphne to Balmoral, Buckingham Palace and Sandringham. But like all writers she drew on what she knew – and many of the characters in her plays and novels are based on her friends, both royal and theatrical.

Through the power of Hollywood studios, the characters that she created have come alive for millions throughout the world. But if we are to discover the real Daphne du Maurier – and the many reasons for her eccentric attitude to life, and her development as a writer – we must return to Daphne's childhood, in London, Paris and Cornwall. These formative years would set the tone for her adult existence.

The key to much of Daphne's private world is her fascinating childhood and adolescence.

2

Childhood and Adolescence

'They seemed old beyond their years, with a queer, half-fledged wisdom picked up from books and odd scraps of gossip; they talked with assurance about things they did not understand ...'   *Gerald*

Daphne du Maurier was born on 13 May 1907, the second daughter of Muriel and Gerald du Maurier. Her upper-class upbringing in Edwardian London, at her parents' home of Cannon Hall in Hampstead, was privileged, almost like that of royalty in its remoteness from harsh realities. Hers was a private world of make-believe and fantasy, populated by famous actors and playwrights and royal personalities, though the du Mauriers were not connected to any of the great English families (unless we count Mary Anne Clarke, who had graced the bed of the Prince Regent's brother). Not only was Daphne's father a celebrated actor, but her mother had also been an actress, Muriel Beaumont; she had given up the stage to look after her family and seems always to have resented this. Not the most loving of mothers, she left the upbringing of her children to a series of nurses and governesses, some of whom Daphne remembered as rather fearsome.

Daphne's grandfather, George du Maurier, had died thirteen years before she was born, but his influence lingered in family tradition, the position he had achieved and the talents his grandchildren inherited. Described by many as 'rather Bohemian', he had been born in Paris in 1834; his mother was the daughter of Mary Anne Clarke, and his father Louis-Mathurin du Maurier, a man of many talents — which unfortunately did not include that of making money. The family moved to London and George (always known within the family as 'Kicky') studied chemistry, which he detested, but on his father's death in 1856 he persuaded his mother to let him return to Paris and study art. He lost the sight of his left eye in the summer of 1858, and for a time feared he would lose the sight of both. But he established himself as an illustrator in London, and on a cold and sunny day in 1863 he married Emma Wightwick, the daughter of a Bond Street linen draper. He illustrated famous novels of the day, including those of Mrs Gaskell, but it was his acceptance of a place on the staff of *Punch* in 1864 which brought him financial security; he sent Gerald, his younger son, to be educated at Harrow (Guy, the elder, went to Marlborough). For thirty years or so the name of du Maurier was a byword for social lampoonery — an observer of people from all walks of life, he took particular pleasure in satirizing fashionable upper-class and middle-class life in his cartoons.

Gerald du Maurier, the last of five children, was born when his father was almost forty. George seems to have been an attentive father, who often took his offspring to the seaside for holidays. Their particular favourite was Whitby, in Yorkshire, and in due course Gerald would encourage his own family to take pleasure in and to feel at home at the coast – first of all in Whitby and then, of course, in the pretty little town of Fowey in Cornwall.

Gerald enjoyed a glittering career. Known as an actor with a genius for creating an 'atmosphere' in any production in which he appeared, he made a reputation in criminal roles, beginning with *Raffles* in 1906. In 1910 he became, like Seymour Hicks and Fred Terry, an actor-manager when he went into theatrical management with a man called Frank Curzon. Together they ran Wyndham's Theatre in London's Charing Cross Road – over the years it was often referred to as 'Gerald's theatre', and it became world famous as the place where he could be seen on stage.

Daphne was the middle of Gerald du Maurier's three children: she had an elder sister, Angela, and a younger, Jeanne. Daphne made up nicknames for herself, her friends and her family – two she could remember when I knew her were 'Screwb' (herself) and 'Pug' (Angela). Each of them inherited the family talent to a greater or lesser extent. Angela went on the stage briefly and then became a writer, Daphne inherited her grandfather's flair for telling a tale and Jeanne his talent for painting.

Described by a childhood friend as 'by far the prettiest of the du Maurier girls', Daphne was as different from Angela and Jeanne as ice is from fire. Angela was delighted to charm her parents, often at glittering soirées of theatrical personalities, and Jeanne had only to smile to captivate them, but Daphne hated social occasions and was never happy except when she was on her own, reading. An intelligent child, she was easily bored with companions of her own age, and as her mental powers developed she turned to adults for excitement or friendship, or to books.

We know that she read *Jane Eyre*, *Wuthering Heights*, and *Treasure Island*: the effect of Stevenson's story is apparent in *Jamaica Inn*, which she wrote when she was in her late twenties, and that of *Jane Eyre* in *Rebecca*, written a couple of years later. Her childhood comments of 'charming' and 'very good' do little to show the depth of the impression these classics made on her. Daphne told me: 'During my childhood, the reading of books became very important to me. I learned to read at a very early age. The characters I read about were acted out by my sisters and me ... during these years I thought it was much more fun to be a boy than a girl, and all my life I have wished that I had been born a boy. I think this attitude has resounded through some of my books.' It is interesting that when in time she did become a writer, the narrators of five of her novels were masculine (she referred to the 'alter ego' who was their author as Eric Avon; like the Brontës with Gondal, she had created her own private world, but one which even as an adult she could still enter).

Daphne's childhood was an enchanted time, with money plentiful. In her own words, Gerald would: 'Give lavish gestures, like take enormous parties of friends on lovely holidays to Cannes, Monte Carlo and Italy. Gerald loved an entourage, and to be the centre of attention. To a certain degree I reacted against this – in some ways this made me more withdrawn and self-absorbed.'

During these formative years, Daphne's world was populated by men and women who were themselves creators of fantasy and make-believe, and many children would have revelled in the theatrical atmosphere. But even from an early age, Daphne was very uncertain of herself and longed for praise and support. She used her imagination to create a private world into which she could escape from the pressure of her luxurious and closely watched everyday life. It is curious that Daphne felt her privileged way of life had been a hindrance to what she really wanted to do as an adult. As a child she was endlessly pampered by her parents, who were – in effect – stifling any talent that she had. She was obedient, and went along with her parents' wishes, but all the same she felt the need to make up and write down stories.

Though completely free from want, and so at the opposite end of the scale from the young writer starving in a garret or struggling to write at the end of a gruelling day's work, she nevertheless found it difficult in her Hampstead home to find the time and privacy to write, to compose properly. It seems to me that in the self-imposed isolation she sought then lay the beginning of her reclusive attitude to life later.

Educated at home by a governess, Miss Waddell ('Tod'), and then at a finishing school in Paris, Daphne passed a childhood unclouded by financial restraint. Most writers are spurred on by the need to earn, but some – like members of the Brontë family – have the need to express their feelings on paper. That is how Daphne enjoyed her life: she lived through her imagination, and the private world and characters that she created.

As a girl she was often sent abroad to stay with rich friends and relatives, and some of these experiences were used later in her short stories and novels. Daphne told me about her beginnings as a writer: 'I started to write when I was about thirteen or fourteen, and I used to scribble short stories. We had a very good governess, Miss Waddell – it was Miss Waddell who really got me started and encouraged me to write. When I was sixteen or seventeen, I went overboard for Katherine Mansfield's short stories and hoped that mine would be as good as hers.

'I also read all of Maupassant in French. When I was eighteen, my uncle – my mother's brother, Comyns Beaumont – who was editor of *The Bystander* was shown some of my stories by my father. Uncle Comyns said, "We must put one or two in *The Bystander*." This was most exciting! He published a short story and a poem.'

Comyns Beaumont also advised Daphne to go to the literary agency of Curtis Brown, where she was taken under the wing of Michael Joseph who encouraged her to write her first novel, *The Loving Spirit*. A childhood friend remembered Gerald du Maurier's reaction to Daphne's success as a writer: 'Gerald was tickled pink, and I think they were tremendous friends. I don't think she could help writing at all, it was something that boiled up inside her ... She just had to write ... Jeanne has inherited a talent for painting, Daphne's was the same.'

Gerald du Maurier was regarded by many of his public as a figure of sheer decadence; he was known to walk around the house wearing silk pyjamas from Beale and Inman of Bond Street, a long cigarette holder in his hand or at his lips. He smoked continually, a habit adopted by Daphne when still quite young, and even franchised his name for use as a cigarette brand. Daphne thought her father to be an adorable character; though he lacked the matinée-idol good looks of, say, Ivor Novello, he was recognized by his daughter as being 'a menace' because he was so attractive, and she told me that she thought 'his inclination to "bits on the side" made him jealous and dampening'.

He had Edwardian values with regard to the upbringing of his family. His daughters learned to be careful what they said and their actions were carefully controlled. Despite his public image, and the change in the moral climate of the 'Roaring Twenties', Gerald was a strict parent. Once his daughters were nubile, they found him to be (in Daphne's words) 'suspicious and investigative'. Boyfriends were not encouraged to attend the Sunday lunch parties at Cannon Hall; if they came once, they never came again. Neither Angela nor Jeanne ever married, and in some ways they became afraid of men. Daphne herself attributed Gerald's attitude both to the era in which he lived, and to his knowledge of his own behaviour within the theatrical world in which he moved.

Daphne discovered, and was told, the facts of life around the age of twelve. She had three relationships in the next ten or so years which were of importance in teaching her about herself and her feelings. The first was with a cousin, Geoffrey du Maurier, who was much older than Daphne; the second was with Carol Reed, later to become famous as a film director, and the third with Mlle Fernande Yvon, *directrice* of the finishing school Daphne attended in Paris.

Geoffrey du Maurier was the son of Gerald's elder brother, twenty-two years older than Daphne and married. He fell in love with her when she was only fourteen, and his crush on her lasted for several fervid years. But for Gerald's intervention, it might have developed further. In later years Daphne told me that Geoffrey was nothing to her; 'he was more like a brother'. She described her feeling for him as like that of Tessa (in Margaret Kennedy's popular 1924 novel, *The Constant Nymph*, which became the stage play that launched John Gielgud's career in 1926) for Lewis Dodd – entirely innocent, but a remarkable liaison with a then-married man.

After this relationship with Geoffrey, the attentions of Carol Reed – a young man of about her own age – proved her real sexual awakening. Her only lover before her marriage, he took her virginity one Friday night in

Hampstead when she was about seventeen. Even so, she was not inclined to marry him.

The du Mauriers enjoyed travelling abroad, and Daphne began an obsessive crush on Mlle Yvon, whom she had first met when she was at finishing school. She appeared poised and fascinating to the younger woman, and they remained friendly until Mlle Yvon's death. Daphne explained it to me: 'My own thing with Fernande was mother/daughter. I had missed that relationship with my mother, as we didn't "click" until Daddy died.' This liaison was an important stage in Daphne's growing-up, and it introduced her to a more sophisticated lifestyle as well as to all things French. The city of Paris and the South of France would reappear in her work in one form or another throughout her career.

Her career started with the publication of a poem and a short story. Gradually poetry gave way to prose, but she was still writing the former when Jesse Lasky Jr met her at Cannon Hall during the 1920s. 'When I was introduced to Daphne, she was in the attic of her Hampstead home, sitting cross-legged and wearing what appeared to be men's trousers. I was keen on writing poetry too, so we exchanged poems ... I noticed that she was not in the least conventional, so I was very surprised, a few years later, when she did the most conventional thing possible – marrying a Guards officer.'

This dual attitude to her personal life would stay with Daphne throughout most of her life, as the actor Michael Gough remembered: 'Most of the time Daphne wanted to be Lady Browning, the lady of the manor and a respectable army wife – but occasionally she behaved like her grandfather, the Bohemian George du Maurier. In this way she lived her life and career.'

In many respects Daphne's childhood was overshadowed

by her father, Gerald, and his larger-than-life personality. Although most of the plays that starred him are hardly ever heard of today, a few have become classics in the theatre – *Dear Brutus* by J M Barrie, for example, which showed Gerald at the peak of his acting powers in 1917, his last appearance on the stage before he quixotically left Wyndham's to join the army in 1918. Barrie was a regular visitor to the du Maurier home, almost part of the family, in fact Daphne and her sisters referred to him as Uncle Jim. A great friend of Gerald's sister Sylvia and her husband, he had written *Peter Pan* in 1904 for Sylvia's boys (Gerald created the part of Captain Hook), and he became their guardian on their father's death. His personality left an indelible mark on the young Daphne, who regarded *Dear Brutus* as his best play.

Gerald du Maurier was renowned as a 'natural' actor, and for the creation on stage of many famous characters. He was the leader of the school of acting that revolted against the flamboyance of Tree and Irving, and that instituted the pre-1939 tradition of underplaying. Not unnaturally, his influence was felt by many, including the up-and-coming young John Gielgud. He told me: 'I never worked with Gerald, professionally anyway. He was great fun. He had a rather Joyce Grenfell/Celia Johnson attitude to the theatre, as though it was an enormous garden party. He was a natural actor, but always letting mousetraps off behind people. He was excellent at creating an atmosphere. Olivier and I both admired him, but I don't think he liked us at all. He rather resented me, and Charles Laughton – I think he felt we were trying to usurp the throne he had occupied for so many years. This was not true.'

Another actor then on the brink of a career that would bring him world-wide fame was Rex Harrison. When I met

him, a few years before his death, he recalled: 'I admired
Gerald du Maurier enormously – he made acting seem so
easy and natural. I think he made you believe that he had
only just popped into the theatre for a spot of acting on the
way to his London club. I have wanted all my life to emulate
Gerald's sophisticated style, and his influence will always
remain with me.'

The du Maurier Sunday lunch parties at Cannon Hall
were special social occasions, gathering in the famous from
the world of the theatre and the cinema. Gerald's first film
appearance, in 1930, was in a Galsworthy story filmed on
Dartmoor, *Escape*, directed by Basil Dean. Family friends
such as Mary Fox (aunt of the actors Edward and James Fox;
her mother appeared on stage with Gerald) were there, and
Douglas Fairbanks Jnr too was a visitor in the 1930s.

'I have fond memories of Cannon Hall and Gerald du
Maurier. He was a wonderful man – he treated me like a
human being and not just a whippersnapper. I remember,
while we were making *Catherine the Great*, he would often
call at my flat in London. It was on these occasions that he
would show me the wind-up toys he had found – he was so
amusing! Gerald also liked to watch children sail their boats
in the park, and he would hand out coins to them.' Sir
Douglas (he was knighted in 1949 for 'furthering
Anglo-American amity') continued: 'When we were filming
Catherine the Great in London, I found they had given
Gerald du Maurier, who had only a small part in the film, a
very small dressing-room, while I (I was playing the Grand
Duke Peter) had the large one next to Elisabeth Bergner,
who was playing Catherine. So I swapped, giving Gerald the
star dressing-room – he never realized this at any time during
the filming. I felt he deserved to be treated like a major star,
even when he had only a small part in the film.

'I got to meet Daphne later in life. She attended some of my dinner parties in London, and I greatly admired her.'

Daphne had never wanted to go on the stage, though she did walk on in a Shakespeare play at the St James's Theatre in her teens and Mary Fox remembers her taking a screen test at a London studio for the film version of *The Constant Nymph*. (When a film version was finally made in 1943, it starred Joan Fontaine, and she received an Oscar nomination.) Daphne's elder sister, Angela, was the only one of Gerald du Maurier's daughters to go on the stage, where she could have had a successful career. She remembered: 'I thought it was hysterically funny when I played Wendy, in *Peter Pan*, because I flew through the air and fell right into the orchestra pit.'

A parent's fame can cause difficulties for children, and in many ways Daphne reacted against the fame of her father. To prove herself she had to break away and find the freedom to create her own life and destiny. But something in her past haunted her – all her life she would try to re-create her childhood. She educated her own children at home, as she had been educated, with the same governess, Miss Waddell, who had taught her. Despite all her travel abroad, and holidays in large houses such as Milton, Daphne found that the location which attracted her more than social life in London, more than glittering parties and dining with the Prince of Wales, was Cornwall.

She had only happy memories of the Duchy, for her visits to Cornwall had been magic moments. Holidays in England had often been spent with famous personalities, such as Gladys Cooper and her young son, John, who were more like family than friends; but it was the playwright Edgar Wallace who had made possible the strength of the du Maurier connection with Fowey. A friend of Gerald,

Wallace had been very generous with the profits from his play, *The Ringer*. Without this extra money Gerald would not have been able to buy Ferryside, the house overlooking Fowey harbour which became the family's holiday home. And it was the inspiration of the little Cornish town, and of the neighbouring village of Polruan, which gave the impetus to Daphne's career as a writer.

All her life, Daphne wrote more about places than about people. As a result, impressions taken as a girl set the tone for her adult life. She told me, 'My childhood and adolescence was an interesting and formative time. I kept no diaries after I married; in fact, I was bored by myself as an adult.' She did write an autobiography, *Growing Pains*, but it dealt only with her youth, telling the reader hardly anything of her adult years.

Daphne grew up a very complicated, perhaps even in some ways confused, person. As a child she had wished to be a boy; as an adult she told several people, 'I would prefer to be a man. If I were, my novels would be more highly thought of.'

Although she was very fond of her sisters, there was rivalry between them. She told me, 'My elder sister writes, you know, but she never had the success I have had. But she tries to write!' In 1951, Angela published a book called *Only the Sister* – so called from an occasion when she was stopped and asked for her autograph, then overheard someone say, 'Oh, it's not her. It's only the sister!'

It is obvious that the coastline, towns and history of Cornwall have intrigued the du Maurier family. From her earliest visits they cast a spell over the life and private world of Daphne du Maurier. She felt at home there, as though she had found her real destiny, maybe because of her French ancestors and the ties between Cornwall and France. For whatever reason, Daphne's visits to Cornwall turned to longer spells and finally to full-time residence in a county she was loath to leave.

3

Cornwall, The Loving Spirit *and* Jamaica Inn

> Alas – the countless links are strong
> That bind us to our clay.
> The loving spirit lingers long
> And would not pass away.
> Emily Brontë

When we examine the career of Daphne du Maurier, an inevitable question arises: 'Why Cornwall?' To answer it we need to look at both the place and the person.

For many, Cornwall feels like a separate place. Maybe it is its remoteness from the capital, London, more than 280 miles away from the county's westernmost town, Penzance. Maybe it is the warm climate and mild winter weather, which encourage vegetation of a luxuriance unknown elsewhere in the British Isles. Maybe it is the long history of the Cornish people, a people with a language of their own, ancient customs and superstitions. Like Scotland and

Ireland, Cornwall has a thread of violence in its historic past which can help the imaginative mind to conjure up visions so clear they are almost real.

Cornwall is an extension of the British Isles in much the same way that Italy is of Europe, and these two peninsulas, so unlike in size, are interestingly similar in shape. Both areas are long and narrow, terminating in a well proportioned claw; both have a river to the north that creates a natural border – in Italy the River Po rises near Monte Visa, and flows to the Adriatic, while the boundary between Cornwall and Devon is the River Tamar. And both Italy and Cornwall have attracted colonies of writers and artists, some of whom have gone on to become world famous.

Writers associated with Cornwall this century include Sir Arthur Quiller-Couch, professor of English Literature at Cambridge (and a friend of the du Mauriers), who wrote *From a Cornish Window*, and, under the pseudonym of 'Q', a series of delightfully humorous novels set in a Cornish background. Howard Spring, author of *Fame is the Spur*, moved to Cornwall in 1939, and Winston Graham, who wrote the Poldark Chronicles, is another writer who made his home in the county and gained fame from works with a background of Cornish history and romance. But perhaps Daphne du Maurier has done most to draw on Cornwall's special qualities. In his book *The Timeless Land, the Creative Spirit in Cornwall*, Denys Val Baker argues that Daphne's relationship to Cornwall has created such memorable work, which stands as a monument to her genius, by giving her real events and a real landscape for her imagination to embellish and weave into dramatic stories.

The du Maurier family, like many other urban families, first came to Cornwall for holidays. As a child, Daphne spent many happy weeks there, visiting most parts of Cornwall with her parents – it was in a small rock pool on Kennack Sands, on the Lizard peninsula, that she learned how to swim – and the coastline and beaches appealed to the du Maurier girls as they would to any children. But it was the historic and peaceful town of Fowey, in south-east Cornwall, which particularly attracted her, as it had attracted other writers (including 'Q', whose success had made it a popular Edwardian resort) before her. Here it was that the nearly grown-up Daphne spotted Ferryside, a house like a Swiss cottage at the edge of the harbour; it needed repair and modernization, but it would be ideal as a retreat from London.

'Fowey,' reflected Sir John Betjeman, 'is a haunted town made for sailors and pedestrians.' It is steeped in history and folklore, and is little changed today, sixty years after Daphne first discovered it. It is still difficult to get in and out of, whether you enter the town through hilly streets which wend their way down toward the river and the harbour, or whether you arrive, as the du Mauriers did, on the Bodinnick car ferry. From this vantage point you can see all the town laid out in front of you, and across the harbour lies the picturesque village of Polruan.

Here Daphne discovered that her private world could be secure. 'When the hired car swept around the curve of the hill,' she told me, 'the full expanse of Fowey harbour was beneath us. The whole vista was like a gateway to another world. Here, I thought, was the freedom I had sought, and not yet found. Here was the freedom and solace to walk, sail, go fishing, and even perhaps to write.'

In earlier centuries, because of its excellent natural harbour and its strategic position guarding the entry to the English Channel, Fowey was an important port. In 1347 it sent as many as forty-seven ships to aid Edward III in his siege of Calais, and during the reign of Elizabeth I the *Francis of Fowey*, a ship owned by the local Rashleigh family (who also owned the houses of Menabilly and Kilmarth, where Daphne would live for so long) sailed with Sir Francis Drake against the Spanish Armada. The sea-going tradition in Fowey and Polruan was still strong when Daphne first visited the place, and she became a keen student of its local history.

Thanks to the author's generosity, Gerald had done very well financially out of Edgar Wallace's play, *The Ringer*, which he'd produced at Wyndham's; as was his custom, he handed over the proceeds to his wife. The result was an investment in the 'Swiss cottage' in Cornwall. Up until then the du Mauriers had rented places for their holidays, and the acquisition of a permanent Cornish base was a major step. Daphne's mother negotiated with the owners, and soon the property had changed hands. This was a bid by Muriel, who had a natural flair for houses and their renovation, to ensure annual holidays that were happy – Gerald was easily bored, and his temper was not improved by his increasing financial worries. Not until everything, down to shrimping nets poised ready in the hall, was in place was he allowed to see Ferryside.

Though he liked it at first, the poor weather of 1928, followed by the failure of two of his plays, set him against it. He would suffer a week or ten days, because his family adored it, but he never really enjoyed it after that first summer.

Daphne had always enjoyed her own company, and the lure of solitude in Fowey was more attractive than all her social pleasures in London. She wrote more about places than about people, and the richness and romance of local legends captured her vivid imagination and stimulated her creative powers. She explored the old town, found that people were reasonably friendly, and listened to the elderly and their stories of forgotten days.

The Duchy's historic past was to give her ideas for many of her books, but the first real inspiration occurred during a walk along Pont Creek, an estuary which separates the villages of Bodinnick and Polruan. On one of her expeditions, Daphne discovered the wreck of an old schooner, the *Jane Slade*, built at Polruan. Once a beautiful vessel, she lay rotting in the mud, with only her figurehead challenging the passing of time. Daphne was intrigued, and began to find out what she could about its history. Until then she had written poetry, short stories and articles, but her interest in the Slade family, who had owned a boat-building yard in Polruan, was the first step towards a full-length novel. When she was given an old box of faded letters which had belonged to the Slades, and many of which went back to the early nineteenth century, she realized that there was enough material for an exciting novel. The Slades became the Coombes – Jane Slade became Janet Coombe – and Polruan became the fictional fishing village of Plyn.

She began writing her first novel on a cold and windy night in October 1929, with the rain lashing against the windows of her bedroom at Ferryside. (Years later, the figurehead of the *Jane Slade*, presented to Daphne in recognition of her status as a writer about Cornwall, would be mounted on a beam outside that bedroom window.) Real Cornish locations were peopled from her imagination, real events were heightened into a gripping story. This use of Cornish people, towns and countryside was a formula to which she would return, and which would eventually bring her world-wide fame. Michael Joseph, the future publisher, whom she'd already met through the literary agency of Curtis Brown, encouraged her in her work on *The Loving*

Spirit and published it in 1931. To her surprise, it became an instant bestseller. (She recorded in *Gerald* that her father was tremendously proud – and furious when no salesman could produce it at a bookstall.)

The title *The Loving Spirit* was taken from a poem by Emily Brontë, and many people have regarded Daphne's books as being rather 'Brontëfied' in their construction, with their use of landscape alongside character descriptions. Certainly Daphne was fascinated throughout her career with this half-Irish, half-Cornish family – the mother of Emily, Charlotte, Anne and Branwell was Maria Branwell, who came from Chapel Street in Penzance. To what extent Daphne's style as a writer was influenced by that of the Brontë sisters is open to debate, but there is a parallel in that they, as she did, merged personal experiences and imagination, and became closely associated with a particular area. They were born in Yorkshire, and it is with that county that they are identified, though neither of their parents was Yorkshire born or bred. Daphne found Cornwall as a child, and felt that she had finally come home. In her book *Vanishing Cornwall*, published in 1967, she highlighted her association with her adopted county – one might almost call it a Cornish autobiography – and devoted a whole chapter to the Brontë family and their Cornish connection.

When she was asked to write a foreword to a new edition of Charlotte Brontë's *Jane Eyre* in the late 1950s, Daphne decided to undertake a biography of Branwell Brontë, and *The Infernal World of Branwell Brontë* was published by Victor Gollancz in 1960. It portrays a man haunted by demons, seeing imaginary luminosities, and suffering from frequent trembling of the limbs. Daphne took the view that he was more likely to have been suffering from fits rather than, as often suggested, from delirium tremens brought about by excessive drinking.

Branwell Brontë's work may not have had quite the same polish and power as that of his famous sisters, but he had a boyhood and youth of staggering productivity. His flame flickered early, brilliantly, so much so that the lives and loves of his imaginary characters burnt him out and by the age of twenty-one his invention was exhausted. He died on a Sunday morning in 1848, aged only thirty-one.

Daphne's careful writing and research portray a sad figure, unfortunately unloved in a contented household, a curious castaway. 'I felt he was the least understood of all the Brontë family. I also remember trying to gain some impression of Branwell's lifestyle and attempting to drink some laudanum with milk – but I gave up and poured it down the sink!'

But to return to 1931: among the rewards that the success of *The Loving Spirit* brought its author was recognition in the eyes of the local community, and admiration from the public. One fan was a young officer in the Grenadiers, reputedly the most handsome man in his regiment, Frederick Browning. (He had served successively as adjutant and as company commander before he came of age; because he looked even younger than his years he was nicknamed 'Boy'; though to Daphne he became 'Tommy'.) He read Daphne's novel, and determined to sail down to Fowey to meet its author.

Frederick Arthur Montague Browning had been born in 1896, the son of Colonel F H Browning. After schooling at Eton, he was commissioned into the Grenadier Guards in 1915. Within a year of arriving at the Western Front he won the DSO for taking command of three companies, whose officers had all been either killed or wounded, during heavy fighting. He also received the French Croix de Guerre, and was mentioned in dispatches. In 1924 he became adjutant of

Sandhurst, where he inaugurated what has since become the tradition of the adjutant mounting the steps of the grand entrance on horseback, and where he was known as the best turned-out officer in the army and a strict disciplinarian. Later, in 1940, he would be chosen to head an experimental airborne formation, which early in 1941 would become the 1st Airborne Division.

When Daphne first met him, 'Boy' Browning was a handsome, dashing figure who soon captured her heart and her imagination, for the male side of her personality would be able to live through her future husband's heroic exploits. In conversation with me she recalled her first glimpse of him from the windows of Ferryside: 'I saw this white motor boat cruising around the harbour, and sister Angela said, "There's a most attractive man at the helm." Later I was introduced to Tommy, as I came to call him, and we both enjoyed one another's company.' This initial meeting led to a courtship, and a few weeks later Daphne and Browning were engaged.

In many ways Gerald had been a heavy-handed father, always quizzing the girls about boyfriends, and trying to put an end to any relationship that might break up his family life – it may indeed be due to these tactics that Angela and Jeanne never married. At all events, when Daphne – his favourite daughter – wrote from Fowey saying that she was going to be married, Gerald burst into tears, saying 'It isn't fair.'

However, he conquered his disappointment and the marriage took place when the sun was high in the sky on a glorious summer Tuesday, 19 July 1932, at the church of Lanteglos by Fowey. Like the Jennifer and John at the end of *The Loving Spirit*, the bride and groom made their way to church by boat, along Pont Creek. Years later Daphne described her wedding to me: 'It was a beautiful day, and both my parents were there.' (However, neither of her sisters was, and – perhaps significantly – it was not her father but her cousin, Geoffrey du Maurier, who performed the rite of giving the bride into the keeping of her husband.) 'After the reception, Tommy and I sailed out in his boat *Ygdrasil*, heading down channel for the Helford River and Frenchman's Creek. Nothing could have been more beautiful.' Again, we find this curious mingling of fact and fiction: a scene she had created in her imagination had become a scene she could now live out.

Her new husband seems to have been as fascinated by the town and harbour of Fowey as Daphne herself had been during her early visits, and after their marriage Daphne continued to spend as much time as she could in Cornwall. The place haunted her. As if touched by ghostly fingers, wherever she was, her thoughts were forever turning back to this beloved county. Many of her books recall its past beautifully, though the historical novel is perhaps one of the most difficult to write: the author is limited by the need to adhere to particular patterns, defined by history, which demand a cetain degree of accuracy.

Daphne once admitted to me: 'It's a difficult business ... The fact is, I have always been interested in the past. The real problem is striking a balance. You've lots of truth to go on, and yet you want to hold the attention of the reader. You play with things a bit, but you hate to go wrong with basic history ... The older I get, the keener I get on the truth. Naturally, though, I take liberties with dialogue – the historical novelist must.'

No one driving over Bodmin Moor and coming suddenly upon the forlorn outline of the Jamaica Inn at Bolventor can fail to feel the impact of its stark, bleak setting even now, and Daphne du Maurier's next well-known Cornish novel owes its genesis to a visit she made there in the 1930s. She had spent many Sunday afternoons at the house of Sir Arthur Quiller-Couch, enjoying tea and talking about the history of the area, and it was his suggestion that Daphne and his daughter Foy should visit the inn.

The two of them left Fowey on horseback early one morning, intending to visit an elderly lady who lived at Trebartha Hall, about four miles east of the historic inn. Difficulties occurred during the journey, and Daphne and Foy found the going strenuous. The countryside was inhospitable and Daphne, not a good horsewoman, soon realized that they would have to spend the night somewhere.

It was evening when they came to Jamaica Inn; they decided to stay there a couple of nights and visit local beauty spots. The next day they explored Dozmary Pool, and the village and church of Altarnun, where they became friendly with the local parson. He called on them that evening, as they were eating the simple evening meal of bacon and eggs provided by the temperance house, and he talked long into the night, sitting beside a large peat fire. He told them about the surrounding area, and the legends associated with Bodmin Moor, and many of these stories found their way into *Jamaica Inn*.

Jamaica Inn was Daphne's fourth novel, for *The Loving Spirit* had been followed by *I'll Never Be Young Again*, the first of her books to be written from a masculine point of view, in 1932 and *The Progress of Julius* in 1933. First published in England during January 1936, *Jamaica Inn* was an immediate popular success, selling thousands of copies in its first year. Much of the story of *Jamaica Inn* has now passed into folklore in the area, and the book is now regarded as one of Daphne du Maurier's classic 'Cornish' works.

The name Jamaica Inn goes back at least to 1789; one theory is that the place is so named because it sold Jamaica rum, but the Cornish historian, H L Dutch, accounts for it as the perpetuation of a satirical comment made because the loneliness and bleakness of its situation is so unlike Jamaica! Arguably the most famous inn in the British Isles, thanks to the success of the du Maurier novel, it is now much changed, with shops, restaurant and bars all named from the novel. And when, following her death, Daphne's possessions were sold at auction in 1990, it was the owner of the inn who bought her writing desk and other personal mementos for display there.

The author's note at the beginning of the book, dated from Bodinnick-by-Fowey, October 1935, states:

> Jamaica Inn stands to-day, hospitable and kindly, a temperance house on the twenty-mile road between Bodmin and Launceston.
>
> In the following story of adventure I have pictured it as it might have been over a hundred and twenty years ago; and although existing place-names figure in the pages, the characters and events described are entirely imaginary.

What had gone into the making of the novel was later remembered thus by Daphne: 'I developed the idea for the novel *Jamaica Inn* during an expedition with my friend Foy Quiller-Couch, when we visited Jamaica Inn on horseback. I had just begun *Treasure Island* as bedtime reading, and that is when the characters began to develop, and the idea of *Jamaica Inn*, with wrecking and smuggling, became clear to me. My meeting with the parson from Altarnun, who had long white hair, helped me to formulate the story and somehow the characters began to develop in my subconscious and I could clearly imagine the vicar in a more sinister role. This is how he became the ringleader in my story *Jamaica Inn*.'

The heroine is the recently orphaned Mary Yellan, who – because of a promise made to her dying mother – leaves her home at the Helford she loves to go and live with her aunt at Jamaica Inn, Bolventor. Mary is horrified to find her once pretty Aunt Patience a 'poor tattered creature ... dressed now like a slattern, and twenty years her age' under the bullying influence of her husband, Joss Merlyn, a giant of a man who is engaged in smuggling, murder and worse.

The story is set mainly in the desolate Jamaica Inn, on the lonely treacherous moors that surround it, and by the cruel seashore, with occasional contrasts of the warmth and friendliness of the Helford river country, or the ordered way of life in the parsonage or big house. Daphne du Maurier's descriptions of the Cornish moors are undoubtedly some of the finest in any writing about that county, and she paints an impressive portrait of Cornwall in the 1800s. The loneliness of the setting permeates the novel, and becomes the loneliness, the fear and isolation that Mary Yellan feels. Like the later *Rebecca*, *Jamaica Inn* deals with a young woman alone in the world, cast adrift in an unfamiliar hostile environment.

Apart from Mary herself, there are few likeable characters in *Jamaica Inn*, but superlative story-telling holds the reader's attention, and wins sympathy for her plight. On her first Saturday night at the inn, sent to bed by her Uncle Joss, she hears strange sounds and, through a crack in her blind, sees strange bundles being carried to and fro. It is like the refrain from Rudyard Kipling's *A Smuggler's Song*:

Them that asks no questions isn't told a lie.
Watch the wall, my darling, while the Gentlemen go by!

But in *Jamaica Inn* none of the smugglers met at the inn is a gentleman, and their activities are more serious than the illicit importation of 'Brandy for the Parson and 'Baccy for the Clerk'. Daphne du Maurier's imagination gave them a gentleman for their ringleader – unknown to them, and for much of the time to the reader and to Mary Yellan herself. Francis Davey, the albino vicar of Altarnun, proclaims himself to be 'a freak in nature and a freak in time'. With his halo of cropped white hair, and his prominent thin nose, he looks to her like a bird: 'Crouched in his seat, with his black cape-coat blown out by the wind, his arms were like wings. Then he smiled down at her, and was human again.' The vicar may have been the ringleader – but in his first appearance he rescues the lost Mary Yellan as she stumbles across the moor at night, and in his second (on Christmas Eve) saves her from a rain-soaked walk of eleven miles back to the inn from Launceston. She is convinced he is her friend, someone who is on the side of right, and it is only when she is taken to his home after the death of her uncle and aunt that his true character emerges. Throughout each of their encounters there is an uneasy undercurrent of his sexual interest in Mary, though nothing explicit is ever said, and he now reveals that he feels he comes from long ago, 'when the rivers and the sea were one, and the old gods walked the hills'. She must go with him, though his is a soul in torment that has sought but not found peace within the Church; his grudge against the age in which he lives has led to his espousing what he sees as the old pagan barbarism – and planning the wrecking of ships with the consequent loss of totally innocent lives.

The fact that Daphne had made the ringleader of her wreckers a devil in a dog collar (though he was no more evil than characters she portrayed in many of her other works) was to lead *Jamaica Inn* into serious problems later.

The success of the novel meant that the film rights were soon sold. They were bought by a new company, Mayflower Pictures, which consisted principally of the German producer Erich Pommer (who had worked with Marlene Dietrich), and the English actor Charles Laughton, who had decided to co-produce his own starring vehicles. *Jamaica Inn* was to be their third production, and they asked Alfred Hitchcock to direct – Laughton and Hitchcock had known each other since the 1920s, and got along fairly well together.

One of Hitchcock's closest friends in the theatre had been Gerald du Maurier, whom he had produced in a 1930s film, *Lord Camber's Ladies*. 'We had a very fine cast,' said Hitchcock, 'with Gertrude Lawrence, a great star in those days, and Sir Gerald du Maurier, the leading actor in London at the time – and in my opinion, the best actor anywhere.'

Hitchcock and Gerald were friendly competitors in many famous practical jokes. Daphne's father had a taste for these, and used them to enliven long runs, setting clockwork mice scuttling about a stage breakfast-table, screened from view of the audience by coffee-pots and toast-racks, or making the cups and saucers jump about by means of strange contraptions he'd invented. He even staged a version of the Chinese water torture, when he arranged for a slow drip to fall on to an unfortunate actor whose part called for him to remain in one place and conduct a very serious conversation for many minutes on end. He was the butt of a classic Hitchcock practical joke, which involved getting a fully-grown work-horse into the du Maurier dressing-room at the St James's Theatre while he was on stage. It was at about this time that Hitchcock gave his 'blue' dinner parties – everything served would be blue. Without any explanation his guests would be offered blue soup, blue trout, blue chicken and finally blue ice cream, accompanied by blue beverages. This taste for practical joking later found its way into many of Hitchcock's films, including *Jamaica Inn*.

Though Daphne and Hitchcock must have come across one another during her teens, he claimed no special affection for her works, but he could see instantly their cinematic possibilities. (Eventually he filmed three: the full-length novels of *Jamaica Inn* and *Rebecca*, and the short story 'The Birds'.) *Jamaica Inn* was a sinister nineteenth-century period piece which had captured the public's attention, set as it was in real Cornish locations – Hitchcock saw its potential, signed Mayflower's contract, and rashly accepted a large advance of several thousand pounds to make the film in England, the last before he left to work in America.

When Clemence Dane, the novelist and playwright whose first, near-classic, play *A Bill of Divorcement* had a success in 1921 which her later works never quite matched, forwarded the first script, Hitchcock felt that the project was a foolish mistake. He pleaded with Pommer to be released from the deal, and even made plans to sell his house in order to repay the advance. Laughton was displeased, and told Hitchcock that if he cancelled the film Pommer would be put on the streets, a poor German refugee condemned to poverty. Hitchcock agreed to tackle the film and he and his wife Alma Reville, a former film editor and script girl who collaborated as a screenwriter on many of his films, worked on a new adaptation, though the final screenplay was by Sidney Gilliat and Joan Harrison (she went on to work with Hitchcock on many other projects, including *Rebecca*).

The film had a star-studded cast which included Emlyn Williams as a wrecker, Leslie Banks as the landlord of Jamaica Inn, Robert Newton as a customs officer and double agent, Maureen O'Hara as Mary Yellan – and Charles Laughton. Laughton had made his début in feature films in 1929, and had won an Academy Award in 1933 for his performance in *The Private Life of Henry VIII*. A brilliant performer with an astonishing range, he was almost exactly the same age as Alfred Hitchcock (thirteen days older, in fact), and like him generously built. They had in common a Catholic upbringing, an English middle-class background, and a love of music (Hitchcock had vivid memories of listening to Laughton's gramophone at his flat in London's Cromwell Road.)

There the similarities between them ended: their life-styles were entirely at variance. Laughton was the flamboyant bisexual, favouring Bohemian patterns of behaviour, while (despite the practical jokes) Hitchcock was the respectable bourgeois family man. He regarded Laughton professionally as 'childish, self-indulgent and undisciplined'. This undisciplined approach was one of the causes of the problems with the adaptation of *Jamaica Inn*. Another was entirely outside the control of anyone – a vicar could not be seen to be engaged in wrong-doing, insisted the powerful Hays Office.

Named after Will H Hays, a former lawyer appointed by the major Hollywood studios in 1922 as the head of the Motion Picture Producers and Distributors Association of America (MPPDA), the office had been created in an effort to improve the image of the industry after widely publicized scandals had led to increasing pressures to bring in some form of film censorship. In 1934 the Hays Office

Joan Fontaine in the 1940 film *Rebecca*. (*By courtesy of Joan Fontaine*)

I interviewed Joan Fontaine at the NFT in 1978.

Joan and Dame Judith Anderson in the famous balcony scene when many of the sinister undercurrents portrayed in the novel become evident on screen.

Milton House near Peterborough (*above*) and Menabilly: these two houses fused together in Daphne's imagination to create her fictional mansion, Manderley, in *Rebecca*.

implemented the Production Code, which forbade the depiction on screen of scenes of passion, adultery, illicit sex, seduction and rape; they were not even to be alluded to unless they were absolutely essential to the plot, and had to be severely punished by the film's end. The sanctity of marriage was to be upheld at all times (although sexual relations were not to be suggested between husband and wife); profanity, vulgarity, nudity, 'lustful kissing', excessive drinking, cruelty to animals or children were all forbidden, and all criminal activity had to be shown to be punished. Studios were required to submit their scripts for approval before beginning filming, and completed films had to be screened for the office and altered if necessary in order to receive a Production Code Seal, without which no film could be distributed in the United States.

In the first instance, it was agreed that Laughton should play one of the central characters in the story, Mary Yellan's dipsomaniac uncle, Joss Merlyn, who runs the Jamaica Inn and appears to be in charge of the smuggling and other illicit deeds. Then, without warning, Laughton decided he wanted to play the real ringleader, the vicar of Altarnun, who preaches good deeds by day and is the cause of ships being lured on to the rocks by night. But because of the Hays Office's refusal to tolerate the idea of a criminal vicar, the storyline had to be altered – the wreckers would be led by the local squire, renamed Pengellan for the film. (In the original novel, the local squire, Mr Bassat, is a magistrate and a man entirely on the side of law and order. He and his wife welcome Mary into their home after all is over, while she decides what to do with the rest of her life.) So the role Laughton would play was changed again.

Jamaica Inn was an indirect introduction to Hollywood for Maureen O'Hara, who played Mary Yellan in this undistinguished black and white movie. Soon after completing her role, and accompanied by her mother (who had been known as the most beautiful woman in Ireland), she went with Charles Laughton to America. There she began her starring career as Esmeralda to his *Hunchback of Notre Dame*. She made a succession of films, and at one stage was called 'The Queen of Technicolor' on account of her glorious red hair. She seldom gives interviews but, after a silence of many years, spoke to me extensively from her Manhattan home.

'I loved working with Hitchcock – we got on well together, because he was half-Irish. I was only about seventeen, and I remember riding the camera trolley with his daughter, Pat, during the filming. It was great fun! The sets were fabulous – they were all built at the studios. Some of the film was made on location in Cornwall, although I did not go along, and some of the wrecking scenes were done in miniature, in a large tank at the studio as I remember. I had not attempted a large-scale film before, but acting is acting, and I had already worked at the Abbey Theatre in Dublin for a few years.

'Meeting Laughton, whom I also got on well with, was a great boost to my career. He wanted to adopt me, because he had never had a little girl of his own! Laughton was looking forward to playing such a character as the vicar. Due to censorship the story had to be changed – the Hays Office said that if a vicar was portrayed on the screen as a criminal, then the film would not be shown in England, or the United States. There were other complications in that the vicar was more interested in the young girl than he should have been, and at that time this could not be shown on the screen, so it had to be changed, and the ringleader of the wreckers had to be changed to another character, that of the local squire. It was not Charles Laughton's fault that the script was changed; that was all due to censorship.'

The script was reworked, and Laughton's character was changed from that of the vicar to that of the squire and Justice of the Peace. Laughton wanted his role to be built up further, so he brought in J B Priestley to write additional dialogue for his character. This extra input to the screen adaptation of *Jamaica Inn* did not mix particularly well with what had gone before, and made Hitchcock even more worried about attempting the film.

Years later he told the French director, François Truffaut: '*Jamaica Inn* was an absurd thing to undertake. If you examine the basic story, you will see it's a whodunnit. It was completely absurd, because the Justice of the Peace, played by Laughton [was the ringleader and] should have entered the scene only at the end of the adventure. Therefore it made no sense to cast Laughton in that key role. Finally I made the picture and although it became a box-office hit, I'm still unhappy over it … Laughton asked me to show him only in close shots, because he hadn't figured out the manner of his walk. Ten days later, he was inspired by the beat of a little German waltz. Laughton wasn't serious, and I don't like to work that way. He wasn't really a professional film man.'

Laughton had problems throughout *Jamaica Inn*, and he only really found his characterization during the later stages of filming. Always a complex character, his sexuality sometimes led to his acting looking overdone and excessive. There was one scene where he had to be thrown downstairs by one of the wreckers, and – much to the amusement of Emlyn Williams – so much had he enjoyed it that he asked at least six times if the burly actor would do it again.

Hitchcock's direction ensured that the sinister elements of the story were well photographed, and he succeeded in evoking the twilight world of wrecking and smuggling through devices such as the faded sign for the Jamaica Inn, creaking eerily as it swung to and fro. But he tried to inject into Daphne du Maurier's serious story his own macabre brand of humour, and on occasions his direction detracted from otherwise convincing scenes.

Because of all the changes in plot and characters, it would seem Hitchcock tackled the film lackadaisically; there were also rumours that Hitchcock and Laughton fell out during production. Perhaps because of these changes and the faults they led to, *Jamaica Inn*, made in 1939, is one of Hitchcock's least-known films – in some ways it is a forerunner for the much more effective *Rebecca*, which would be his first American film under his new contract with David Selznick. On its release, however, because of the interest the novel *Jamaica Inn* had already aroused, the film was a considerable box-office success. This further enhanced the author's reputation, and paved the way for her not inconsiderable success in the United States as a writer.

For many years Daphne du Maurier herself preferred to forget about this film adaptation of *Jamaica Inn*. She did not understand why the storyline had been changed, and the power of her best-selling novel reduced – she blamed Laughton and Hitchcock because she thought they had quarrelled during filming. She had turned down the opportunity to write the screenplay, though later she wished she had played a role in the production of the film.

'I was not consulted,' she told me. 'I thought the wrecking scene at the beginning good, but I think they could have done a lot more with the story. In fact, they changed the theme, and this affected the plot and the power of my original novel.'

Daphne du Maurier and Cornwall are linked together in many people's minds, and she has been fortunate in that a high percentage of her work has been transferred to the screen, and turned into outstanding films. This film treatment has caused her, too, to pass into Cornish history – and folklore. Her vivid use of real places and settings – such as Jamaica Inn, Frenchman's Creek and Fowey – in the stories she invented and in those she borrowed has given them new legends, new tales of mystery and intrigue.

She found Cornwall to be a limitless source of ideas for future novels. The area's legends and fascinating history encouraged her to write about it more tellingly and with greater conviction than any other writer of her generation. She realized that Cornwall had box-office potential, not just in her own country but in America, too. Although the film treatment of *Jamaica Inn* had not been as she would have wished, her forthcoming novel *Rebecca* would bring her work to world-wide attention, and further film adaptations.

4

Rebecca

> 'Last night I dreamt I went to Manderley again. It
> seemed to me I stood by the iron gate leading to
> the drive, and for a while I could not enter ...'
>
> *Rebecca*

The famous opening line of Daphne du Maurier's novel *Rebecca* has a sinister, haunting melancholy that leads straight to the spirit and the centre of her private world. If she had written just this one work she would still be remembered as a truly great story-teller, for it is with this novel more than any other that she is identified. None of her others has *Rebecca*'s power and strength. It has been outstanding at six levels of entertainment: as a best-selling novel, a radio series, a Hollywood motion picture, a stage play, as a television series and even as an opera.

The content of *Rebecca* and the Freudian subtext of this novel are embodied in a gothic romance. It contains most of the typical trappings of that form: a mysterious haunted mansion, violence, murder, a sinister villain, sexual passion, a brooding landscape, a spectacular fire and the vision of a madwoman at the top of the stairs. But as well as being one of the first major Gothic romances of the twentieth century, and one of the finest yet written, it is also a profound and fascinating study of an obsessive personality, of sexual dominance, lesbianism, and the liberation of one's hidden identity.

As a book, *Rebecca* is one of the great bestsellers in the history of publishing, read and enjoyed in many languages all over the world. First published in England in 1938, it was an immediate popular success, selling thousands of copies and being reprinted many times in the first year. Later that same year it was published in the United States, where it was also acclaimed. 'Daphne du Maurier has written a modern-day *Jane Eyre*,' wrote one critic, while the reviewer in the *New York Times* gave it the ultimate: 'An outstanding novel. I couldn't put it down.'

The story is told by its heroine, who was a gauche young girl, companion to the odious and vulgar Mrs Van Hopper, when she met sophisticated and mysterious Maximilian de Winter holidaying on the French Riviera, apparently trying to recover from the death of his beautiful wife, Rebecca. A whirlwind romance developed; Maxim married the girl, and they returned to his family home, Manderley, in Cornwall. Here the nervous bride, suddenly elevated to the status of mistress of the household, finds herself confronted by the sinister Mrs Danvers, the housekeeper. Mrs Danvers had loved and adored Rebecca ('I did everything for my lady'), and as time goes on the new Mrs de Winter becomes terrified of her – she keeps the rooms used by Rebecca, particularly the bedroom in the west wing with all her clothes, exactly as they had been when she was alive.

Walking around the grounds of Manderley, the narrator

discovers a beach house where Rebecca once entertained her friends. (It will be here, later, that Maxim will confess to her his true feelings for Rebecca, and that he killed her.) There is to be a fancy dress ball, and Mrs Danvers advises her to wear a dress copied from one of the family portraits. Unwittingly, she therefore appears at the ball dressed exactly as Rebecca had been, and Maxim is furious. During the party a boat is wrecked in the bay; divers go down and another boat is found – it is Rebecca's, and her body is still in the cabin. There is an inquest, and Maxim must explain how he came to identify someone else's body as that of Rebecca. A verdict of suicide is reached but her cousin, Jack Favell, with whom she had been having an affair, does not believe it and tries to blackmail Maxim over her murder. Through Mrs Danvers it is discovered that on the day of her death Rebecca had consulted a doctor in London, using an assumed name. Favell, Colonel Julyan (the local magistrate), Maxim and his wife track down the doctor, who explains that Rebecca had cancer which would have killed her within a matter of months. The verdict of suicide thus seems correct.

Favell is not satisfied; and one is left with the understanding that he telephones Mrs Danvers at Manderley and that she sets fire to the house. As Maxim and his wife drive homeward through the night they see what looks like the first red streaks of sunrise, but in the west. 'It's in winter you see the northern lights, isn't it?' she asks. 'Not in summer.'

'That's not the northern lights,' is his chilling reply, 'that's Manderley.'

Millions of readers have taken this story to heart, identifying strongly with the predicament of the second wife who seems to have nothing, not even a name, of her own and is forever overshadowed by the menacing ghostly omniscient presence of the dead Rebecca. *Rebecca* is classic story-telling, with the author revelling in the atmosphere she has created and sweeping the reader along with her gripping narrative.

Daphne did not tell many people, or explain to her public, her reasons for writing this novel, but it can almost be regarded as an autobiography in disguise – not only her private thoughts but also her personal experiences went into the story. Joan Fontaine, who played the second Mrs de Winter in the film version of *Rebecca* (which Daphne admired), told me, 'During the filming the nameless heroine was often referred to as Daphne. In fact, when I told her this many years later in Cornwall she agreed, and told me this was something like the truth, and that she was the girl in the story.'

Though a few close friends knew some of what lay behind it, for many years she tried to ignore the fact that aspects of the novel are sensational. The relationship between Mrs Danvers and the dead Rebecca (who called her 'Danny') has lesbian undertones, something recognized by both Joan Fontaine and by Joanna David, who played the second Mrs de Winter in the 1979 BBC television adaptation of the novel.

Both from her time in Paris and from the circles she moved in in London, Daphne was aware of homosexuality. It is evident from some of her other writings, such as her 1934 novel *I'll Never Be Young Again*, that the influence of Paris (where she spent some wonderful times in the 1920s) stayed with her for many years. It is a city which has for centuries attracted the Bohemian and the artistic, and which accepts unconventional behaviour tolerantly.

During her years in Paris Daphne had as a friend a girl who preferred her own sex. Their friendship was the more important to her because, until after Gerald's death, Daphne did not feel close enough to her own mother to enjoy a warm mother-daughter relationship. This unnamed female friend, with whom Daphne had shared an apartment and sampled Paris nightlife, was very disturbed – on Daphne's return to London she committed suicide by hanging herself from a beam in the apartment which they had shared. This left the impressionable young woman with the knowledge that unconventional relationships can wreak havoc in other people's lives. In fact, one of her earliest short stories, 'No Motive' (written in the 1920s, before she became famous) deals with an unexplained suicide.

Daphne had this to say: 'I would never disapprove of any physical relationship between two women, because I don't disapprove of anything. But I would think it a feeble substitute for married life, and something to get over in youth.' I discussed the story of *Rebecca* with her on several occasions, and she agreed that Mrs Danvers was a sinister character who could quite possibly have enjoyed a lesbian relationship with her beloved Rebecca, and that this would have deeply affected her attitude towards the new Mrs de Winter. She did not air this sensational theory in public, but during her own adolescent years Daphne had known such a woman. In her teens she had mixed with a very open-minded and somewhat Bohemian crowd, to whom the idea that a girl was 'quaint' was perfectly acceptable – as it was to most of the theatrical circle, and to the literary world, of the 1920s and 1930s.

Rebecca also dealt with other topics with which Daphne was herself familiar, such as jealousy and insecurity. She merged many of her own experiences and fears and wrote them in alongside her own imagination. When I knew her, for all her fame, she had a deep-rooted diffidence and was constantly assailed by doubts, causing her to be deeply insecure and to seem at times anti-social.

After her marriage in 1932 to her handsome soldier husband, 'Boy' Browning, she soon discovered that there had been other women in his life – women who mattered, and this greatly perturbed her. One day she opened the drawer of a cupboard in the drawing-room and found a bundle of letters tied together by a blue ribbon. Daphne took the letters out of the drawer and rather nervously began to read them – an act which left her feeling guilty and somewhat embarrassed. She had found the love letters, carefully preserved, written to her husband by his former fiancée, Jan Recardo. A strikingly beautiful débutante, she was to be the model for the character of Rebecca. (Maxim de Winter was based on her own husband – the revolver he uses is a military one, a Smith and Wesson.)

As Daphne looked at Jan Recardo's strong and confident handwriting, very different from her own spidery hand which seemed to reflect her real self with all her doubts and insecurities, the contrast between 'Rebecca' and the young mousy heroine was born. Early in the story she opens a book that does not belong to her and reads 'Max—from Rebecca. May 17th' in 'a curious slanting hand ... the name Rebecca stood out black and strong, the tall and sloping R dwarfing the other letters.' Rebecca's writing, Rebecca's desk, Rebecca's diary, Rebecca's last note to her cousin combine to make a theme which runs through the novel.

In terms of its construction, *Rebecca* is an interesting mixture of fact and fiction. The house, Manderley, which lies at the heart of the story, is a combination of two real houses: Milton, near Peterborough, the ancestral home of the Fitzwilliam family, and Menabilly, the ancestral home of the Rashleigh family near Fowey in Cornwall, which Daphne would live in from 1943 to 1969. She once showed me a photograph of Milton and said, 'There, that is

Manderley.' In fact, she had visited Milton twice when she was a child, and the place must have made a tremendous impression for the memory of those two visits stayed with her all her life. Some of the rooms were not in use, the furniture shrouded in dustsheets, just as the second Mrs de Winter finds part of Manderley to be.

At that time the atmosphere at Milton would have been very formal and correct; there would have been a full house and a staff of butler, housemaids, cook and housekeeper, and all would have known their place. During 1917 the housekeeper there was a Miss Parker, described by Lady Fitzwilliam as 'tall, dark, brooding and very commanding'. It is interesting that in *Rebecca* the housekeeper plays such an important and significant role.

Daphne recalled: 'I had seen the black dress and chain, similar to the one I described Mrs Danvers wearing in *Rebecca*, on a housekeeper in one of the houses I stayed at. It could have been Milton or another house, all I remember of Miss Parker is that she was indeed a severe and rather frightening person. The rest of the description of Mrs Danvers is imaginary.'

The rooms at Milton, and several of the famous portraits by Van Dyck, were used by Daphne in the description of the interior of the fictional Manderley. 'The entrance hall at Milton is exactly as I described in *Rebecca*, when the second wife arrives for the first time at Manderley, and meets the household staff. The only difference is that I gave it a sweeping staircase coming down into the hall, which at Milton I don't think exists.'

The setting for the novel is largely the grounds around Menabilly, though here again imagination comes into play. Daphne transplanted to the Menabilly setting a large house, similar to Milton, but retained the beach house in the cove below Menabilly – this became the beach cottage described so vividly. Marked on Ordnance Survey maps as Pol-ridmouth Bay, but called by Daphne, as by the locals, Pridmouth Bay, it is the setting for Rebecca's murder and the wreck of her boat.

Daphne told me: 'Years ago, when I first visited Fowey, I walked across to Pridmouth Bay and there I saw a boat wrecked on the beach. Years later, whilst living abroad, I would use this and other memories to construct my novel, *Rebecca*.'

Daphne and her sister Angela first came across a mention of Menabilly in an old guidebook, not long after the du Maurier holiday home of Ferryside had been bought. They were still 'new folk from London ... seeing what should be seen', exploring round about Fowey with their friend Mary Fox. The house was three miles or so from the harbour, and to get to it they needed to walk down a long, overgrown drive from the entrance at Four Turnings, just outside Fowey. On their first attempt they did not reach the house; Angela found the journey too much for her, and it was growing dark, so the sisters and Mary decided to return home.

It was this abortive journey along the uncared-for drive, twisting and turning and apparently impassable, that Daphne was to describe in the poignant beginning to her novel: 'Last night I dreamt I went to Manderley again ... The woods crowded, dark and uncontrolled, to the borders of the drive. The beeches with white, naked limbs leant close to one another, their branches mingled in a strange embrace, making a vault above my head like the archway of a church.'

Months later, in the following spring, following a fisherman's chance remark, Daphne rose early, rowed herself across the harbour and found a different way through the woods to discover her house of secrets, the elusive Menabilly. It gave her a new love in her life, and it inspired her to write – not just *Rebecca*, but other Cornish novels such as *Frenchman's Creek* (published in 1941), *The King's General* (1946) and *My Cousin Rachel* (1952). After this discovery of Menabilly, in those days neglected and covered in ivy, Daphne would, in her own words, 'trespass for hours at a time' and imagine the place as it must have been when it was occupied: 'What little blue-sashed, romping children once bestrode [the great dappled rocking-horse with scarlet nostrils]? Where was the laughter gone? Where were the voices that had called along the passages?'

After some thought she wrote to the owner of the house, asking for permission to walk in the Menabilly grounds, and her request was granted. It was, of course, more than the house which fascinated her. There was, too, the history of the Rashleigh family who had owned it for generations. This family was destined to appear again and again, in one disguise or another, in her novels. Further strands for *Rebecca* were gained from her friends, the Quiller-Couches, who told her about one Rashleigh who had been married to a very beautiful wife, whom he had divorced, before marrying a much younger, inexperienced woman. Daphne wondered how the second wife had felt about her predecessor, whether she had been jealous, as she would have been jealous if her husband had been married previously. Would Jan Recardo have been better at cocktail parties than she was?

In 1937 Browning was commanding officer of the Second Battalion, Grenadier Guards, and stationed in Alexandria. Daphne had gone with him, leaving her two small daughters in England in the care of a nanny, with two grandmothers to see that all was well. She was thirty, homesick for Cornwall, bored by army cocktail parties, and she wanted to write. Maybe it was distance and longing that sharpened her memory and imagination, but the fact is that the famous words which open the novel were written in Egypt, not England.

Returning to England with her husband, they were stationed at Aldershot, where they rented a house called Greyfriars, near Fleet. This is where she completed *Rebecca*.

Daphne told me: 'I began the novel in the first person and I avoided giving the heroine a name because it became an interesting exercise in writing and technique.'

Upon publication the novel became an instant bestseller. Serialized in US newspapers it whetted readers' appetites for more, the film rights were sold, and a successful American edition followed later in the year. Daphne du Maurier was an author to be reckoned with – though her old friend Arthur Quiller-Couch prophesied correctly that the critics would never forgive her for *Rebecca*'s success.

The film of *Rebecca* opens with a journey down the deserted drive to the mysterious house of Manderley, which is swathed in Cornish mist, and it becomes very clear that none of the characters in the story are what they seem.

In fact, what the often-filmed Daphne du Maurier brought to the American screen, via Alfred Hitchcock, was fundamentally a landscape – one that's both exterior and interior, both haunted and haunting. Hitchcock's treatment of her work, especially *Rebecca*, changed the way Hollywood treated English romantic literature – just compare this Hollywoodized Cornwall of mind and memory with the Yorkshire moors of *Wuthering Heights*, released in 1939.

The psychological aspect of the story of *Rebecca* seems to me to have influenced the direction of Hitchcock's later

The boat-house beneath Menabilly became Rebecca's cottage in the novel, where she was supposed to have been murdered.

The drawing-room at Menabilly became the Long Gallery, as described in *The King's General*. (*Camera Press*)

Joan Fontaine in the 1943 film version of *Frenchman's Creek*. She starred in it with Basil Rathbone, one of Daphne's early film idols.

The *real* Frenchman's Creek. This idyllic and remote setting on the Helford River was where Daphne and Tommy spent their honeymoon.

Margaret Lockwood (*above*) as
Fanny Rosa in the 1945 film
Hungry Hill. This was the only film
that Daphne attempted to write the
screenplay for. On its release,
Daphne said that the stills were far
more interesting than the final
film.

The Lady of Manderley on the staircase at Menabilly. The portrait to the left is of her father, Gerald, by Philip Streatfeild, and that on the right is of Daphne as a young child. (*Popperfoto*)

films – though he has never admitted this influence in any of the many interviews he has given. What is certain, though, is that Daphne du Maurier's *Rebecca* has become a part of modern romantic legend.

It was Kay Brown, assistant to the film producer David Selznick and who would later discover Ingrid Bergman, who hurried a synopsis to him in May 1938, as soon as the success of the English edition of the book was apparent. She commented:

'... the book has good writing and dramatic scenes that lead into a rather hysterical plot. The fact that it is a melodrama isn't so much against it – after all, melodrama has been responsible for some box office classics – but the fact that the hero definitely murders his first wife, no matter how understandable it is in the story, makes it difficult from the censorship angle. Aside from this there are good roles for Ronald Colman and Carole Lombard.'

At this time, as well as working on the film of *Gone With the Wind* Selznick was trying to find a film role for Colman so that he could wind up his contract with him (Colman had appeared in several Selznick productions, including *A Tale of Two Cities* and *The Prisoner of Zenda*). After reading the synopsis of *Rebecca*, Selznick was sure the part of Maxim de Winter would be perfect for the English actor and wired Kay Brown to 'find out proposed price and further information as to likely sales of the book. I will give further thought to the censorship problems.'

As *Gone With the Wind* showed on its release in 1939, Selznick was an expert at selecting property with potential. He reasoned that *Rebecca* had 'tremendous appeal for women ... and it really is great box office.' The only other criticism, apart from the murder angle, was the title. 'It is difficult to think of calling a picture *Rebecca*,' he

commented,'unless it was made for the Palestine market.'
This was not a joke; he offered to give Doubleday, Daphne's
American publishers, more money for the rights of the book
if they would change the title. They refused but, despite this,
he told Kay Brown to buy the book anyway; the film rights
became Selznick's during the middle of 1938 for around
£10,000.

Following publication in America in September, *Rebecca*
was indeed a success. Spurred on by good reviews and
word-of-mouth comments, it sold close to two hundred
thousand copies in the first few months after publication. If
Selznick had been spoiled by the incredible sales of Margaret
Mitchell's novel, nevertheless the sales of *Rebecca* pleased
him.

During the following months, Selznick paid only passing
attention to *Rebecca* because he was busy getting *Gone With
the Wind* ready to go before the cameras. By now Ronald
Colman, for whom Selznick had bought it, had reservations
about the part of Maxim de Winter. Selznick related this in a
letter to a friend, Jock Whitney:

'Years ago Colman would have welcomed *Rebecca*, but
now with fewer pictures, and his own say about stories, he is
hesitant to do it ... He feels that the things that Max de
Winter is called upon to do would prejudice his public
against him ... He is also fearful about the murder angle and
the possibility of the picture emerging as a woman's starring
vehicle ... We also discussed making the murder of Rebecca
a suicide instead, and as we talked Colman became more
enthusiastic.'

At this time many of the great stars of Hollywood were
very aware of their public images and would do nothing on
screen to damage them. Colman was no different from many
others, and over the next few months he and Selznick would

play 'ring around *Rebecca*' while the producer was completing the film of *Gone With the Wind*.

However, Alfred Hitchcock was now under contract to Selznick Studios. Many English directors were coming to work in Hollywood because of the availability of large studios, and the money to be made there. Hitchcock had come a long way since he had first worked with a Selznick: he had been co-writer and art director on a 1924 British production by Myron Selznick, *The Passionate Adventure*. By 1937 he was probably the most prominent director in the British film industry, a position he had achieved with a string of successes such as *The Lodger* and *Blackmail*.

It was his mastery of the thriller movie, however, that brought him international prominence, from *The Man Who Knew Too Much* in 1934 to *The Lady Vanishes* in 1938. He had developed a highly stylized visual form of direction, and made films with vagaries of plot and sudden sharp twists. The nature of his films, where no one was to be trusted and nothing was as it seemed, may have stemmed from his severe Jesuit training as a child.

Through Myron Selznick, Hitchcock was offered – and accepted – a contract that would pay him forty thousand dollars a picture. As soon as he'd finished work on the lacklustre *Jamaica Inn*, he set sail for Hollywood in late March 1938, accompanied by his wife, Alma, and their daughter, Pat. He believed that his first American project was to be a film based on the disaster of 1912, *The Sinking of the Titanic*. Selznick had made plans to purchase a liner, the *Leviathan*, to use as a stand-in for the doomed *Titanic*, but rising costs caused this project to be dropped.

By chance, Hitchcock decided that *Rebecca* would be ideal for his Hollywood début. Selznick had the rights; he was under contract to Selznick; what could make more sense?

However, the news that he was to direct *Rebecca* did not exactly fill its author with excitement. Kay Brown wrote to Selznick:

'Daphne du Maurier is weeping bitter tears over what happened to *Jamaica Inn*, and she is hoping *Rebecca* isn't going to turn out as big a disappointment.'

'It is my intention,' Selznick wrote, reassuring Daphne, 'to do *Rebecca*, and not some botched-up semi-original, as was done with *Jamaica Inn*.'

Hitchcock and Selznick carried on a series of lengthy meetings regarding the screen treatment of *Rebecca*, which presented various problems, including that of having the story narrated by its nameless young heroine. This was possibly the first time that cinema had attempted a first-person narrative. Selznick allowed Orson Welles to do a radio dramatization of the novel on his 'Mercury Theatre on the Air' in December 1938, at a time when the United States was still recovering from his dramatization of H G Wells's *The War of the Worlds*. Intended by Welles as a Halloween joke, the vivid description of an invasion by space creatures had been so realistic that thousands of listeners had fled their homes in panic.

Selznick gave the following reasons for allowing the broadcast: '*Rebecca* was not receiving sufficient publicity, considering its sensational success as a book. Welles, who is very much in the public eye, would attract more attention, and I was particularly intrigued to hear how he would handle this first-person method of telling the story.'

Hitchcock began working on the script of *Rebecca* with Joan Harrison and Philip Macdonald, but there were further difficulties. A memo from Selznick to Hitchcock:

'It's up to you to decide whether the girl's character should have humour or not ... In endeavouring to transcribe such a character to the screen something might have to be substituted for the first person telling the story ... It might also be necessary to see "Rebecca", but on the other hand it would be better to feel her presence rather than to see her.'

Daphne heard from her agents what was happening in Hollywood, and again she was worried that the film of this, her most successful book so far, would be another disaster. She toyed with the idea of travelling to America to oversee the production of the film, but she had two small daughters and other personal commitments. War clouds were gathering in Europe, her husband was a soldier who would be needed, and it would do nothing for their marriage if she was thousands of miles away in California.

She wrote to David Selznick: 'I greatly hope that you will not resurrect the dead wife ... my conviction is very strong that once this beautiful young woman is shown, the contrast between her and the rather plain and dull second wife would kill the latter.' Selznick reassured her, agreeing that no actress alive could satisfy everybody's conception of what Rebecca would have looked like.

Eventually, in early June 1939, Hitchcock delivered his first draft screenplay to Selznick, who read it and discovered that Hitchcock had diverged widely from the novel. He sent a further memo to Hitchcock:

'I am shocked and disappointed beyond words by the treatment, it is a distorted and vulgarized version of a provenly successful work ... We bought *Rebecca* to make *Rebecca*. I don't think I could create anything as good as the characters and situations of du Maurier's *Rebecca* ... I want this company to produce her *Rebecca*, not an original scenario based upon it ...'

Hitchcock had no option but to deliver another treatment, and he and Alma, with another writer, Michael Hogan, pulled enough good scenes out of the novel to tell the story as Selznick thought it should be told. Robert E Sherwood, who had been awarded the 1936 Pulitzer prize for his play *Idiot's Delight*, suddenly became available as a dialogue writer, and Selznick hired him to revise the dialogue, which was based closely on the original novel.

The murder in *Rebecca* proved tricky, because of the Motion Picture Code and the restrictions of the Hays Office, which declared that no murderer should go unpunished. Colman still had reservations about the project, and for the next few months Selznick was trying to persuade Colman to play Maxim de Winter, and the Hays Office to allow him to retain Daphne's storyline. Despite all his entreaties, the Hays Office emerged triumphant. The murder of Rebecca had to be rewritten so that it became an accident.

'The whole story of *Rebecca* is the story of a man who has murdered his wife,' declared Selznick in exasperation, 'and it now becomes the story of a man who buries a wife who was killed accidentally.' Ronald Colman finally made up his mind, and decided against accepting the role of Maxim de Winter – he told Selznick that he was no longer interested in the projected movie.

Selznick and Hitchcock now had to consider other actors, and their first choice was William Powell. Though he was keen to accept the part, he was under contract to MGM and so not free to do so. Selznick therefore decided to approach Laurence Olivier, whom he'd known since his RKO days when Olivier had been hired because of his resemblance to Ronald Colman.

Olivier's first Hollywood visit had not been a great success; in fact, his then wife, Jill Esmond, was the bigger star. He had returned to England disillusioned, and had concentrated on developing his craft as an actor both on stage and screen. His fast-growing reputation had reached Hollywood, and in late 1938 he was there again, this time to portray the role of Heathcliff in Samuel Goldwyn's production of Emily Brontë's *Wuthering Heights*. Under the excellent direction of William Wyler, Olivier gave a performance that, in the words of one critic, was 'dark, brooding, Byronic and totally convincing'.

In early June 1939 Selznick signed up Olivier for the role of Maxim de Winter, and almost immediately began to do battle with the actress Vivien Leigh. This was despite the fact that she had landed the most sought-after part in Hollywood, that of Scarlett O'Hara in his *Gone With the Wind*. She had accompanied her lover, Olivier, to Hollywood with the hope that they would eventually work on a picture together; now she wanted to play the nameless heroine of *Rebecca*. When Daphne heard this news, she wrote to friends:

'No matter how much I love Vivien, she will be totally unsuitable for the role of I de Winter. If Rebecca herself had lived, Vivien would be my ideal for that character.'

The casting of the mousy second wife had always struck Selznick as a problem. 'The part was considered to be the biggest plum in years, second only to Scarlett O'Hara,' he explained – of course it was sought after. One actress he considered was Margaret Sullivan, whose husky voice had captured the public's imagination in several successful films. In her favour was the fact that she had already played the part in Orson Welles's radio broadcast. Another possible was Olivia de Havilland, who had impressed Selznick with her performance in *Gone With the Wind*. Or what about her sister, Joan Fontaine? Loretta Young would be easy to deglamorize, and might be a good bet. Finally, on the strength of a recommendation from Kay Brown, a new actress named Anne Baxter was tested, and she gave what Selznick considered the most touching test.

Still he was undecided. Perhaps not Olivia de Havilland – it had been so difficult obtaining her from Warner Brothers for *Gone With the Wind*, and she was very reluctant to do a test, particularly when she discovered that Joan Fontaine was also being considered.

Interestingly, Joan had been indirectly responsible for Olivia de Havilland's obtaining the role of Melanie in *Gone With the Wind*. Joan had been working in Hollywood for some time, and her biggest break had come when she was offered the role of Fred Astaire's dancing partner in *Damsel in Distress*. (This was an apt title, for she really was not up to any of the demands made on her.) However, while she was at RKO she caught the eye of George Cukor, then director of *Gone With the Wind*, who asked her to come and test for the part of Melanie.

Joan Fontaine told me: 'I arrived in George Cukor's office, dressed in a claret velvet suit and swathed in furs. Cukor exclaimed, "You're too chic. Melanie must be a plain, simple Southern girl." So I suggested he try my sister, Olivia de Havilland!'

But Joan had impressed Cukor, who detected underneath her sophistication a vulnerability and innocence that he was to use in the film he made after he was fired from *Gone With the Wind*, *The Women*. After her success in this picture, Cukor recommended her to Selznick for the role in *Rebecca*, and while he was testing the other actresses Selznick kept bringing her back for more tests.

Though, under his direction, Joan gave one of the few convincing tests, Hitchcock still felt that too much work would be needed with her and that Margaret Sullivan was the girl for the part. Selznick had almost decided to forget about Fontaine when Cukor told Hitchcock that if he were doing the film, he would certainly use her. Over Labor weekend Selznick paced the floor of his office in Hollywood, trying to come to a decision. At last he picked up the telephone and made a call.

Joan told me, 'It wasn't long after I'd married Brian Aherne, and we were on our honeymoon. I was out on the lake, fishing with Brian, when the phone rang! When I told him I had the part – "I've got Rebecca!" – he turned to me and said, "I shall be busy doing a picture with Carole Lombard, so why don't you do the movie for hat money?" '

As the production of the film got under way, the troublesome problem of finding a house to represent the fictional Manderley must have reminded Selznick of his search for a model for Tara in *Gone With the Wind*. Selznick felt that Manderley was almost as important a character in the film of Rebecca as any of the people. A second unit was sent to England to do some background research, but none of the houses satisfied either Hitchcock or Selznick. However, someone did visit Milton House.

Manderley had to be shown in different conditions: in the rain, at night, looking warm and inviting by day – and it had to be destroyed by fire. The only solution to all their problems was to build miniatures of different sizes. The largest was built first, and cost around twenty-five thousand dollars.

'Interestingly,' I was told by Joan Fontaine, 'Manderley did not exist. All the long shots of the house were painted on glass to give the illusion of a house at different times of the day.'

For various reasons, it was not the happiest of films to work on. Many actors, especially those who had achieved a degree of success on the stage, still regarded making films as rather beneath them. The cast of *Rebecca* included Olivier, already acknowledged as a Shakespearean actor, Judith Anderson, who had played Lavinia Mannon in *Mourning Becomes Electra*, Gertrude in *Hamlet* and Lady Macbeth, Gladys Cooper, a star of the legitimate British stage. Hitchcock was half Irish with a Cockney accent, and these luminaries (and lesser mortals) with their precise enunciation and proper pronunciation made fun of him as he described what he wanted from them and suggested ways of achieving it.

At last, in early September 1939, Hitchcock directed the first shots of *Rebecca*. Five days earlier, on 3 September, England (and France) had declared war on Germany. This made all the English members of the cast eager for news of their relatives at home, and the atmosphere on the set became funereal, full of doom and gloom. In Laurence Olivier's words, 'We all felt our world was coming to an end with the onset of the war. While I was making *Rebecca*, all I could think of was how long it would take me to get home ... Looking back, though, without my success in *Rebecca*, I would never have become an international film star.'

During the production of the film, Joan went down with flu; and while the first unit was closed down, the two second units were at work on location at Del Monte, up in California, near the coast of Monterey. Here they filmed the exterior scenes of the approach to Manderley, and the estate and grounds. The exterior beach scenes were shot at Catalina Island, using doubles for Fontaine and Olivier.

Discussing the making of the film, Joan Fontaine told me: 'There was tension on the set of *Rebecca*. I did not get on with Larry Olivier or any other member of the cast. Olivier made it obvious to me that he actually wanted Vivien Leigh to play my character. In fact, most of the cast kept their distance, but this helped me to create the character of the mousy, frightened second wife.'

The tension rose to a peak one day when Olivier fluffed his lines and cursed in a most ungentlemanly fashion. 'Watch it, Larry,' warned Hitchcock. 'Joan's a new bride.' Olivier, of course, knew that perfectly well, but asked Hitchcock to whom Joan was married. Brian Aherne, Joan told him. 'Couldn't you do better than that?' retorted Olivier, insultingly. (His animosity seems to have lasted. In his autobiography, *Confessions of an Actor*, published in 1979, he refers to Joan as a cow.)

It is hardly surprising that their romantic scenes were not as convincing as they might have been: Olivier's true feeling for Joan shows through in them. His portrayal of Maxim, the lost, haunted hero of Daphne's book, succeeded only through his sheer charm, his Byronic good looks and his carefully modulated voice which combined to mislead audiences into believing that chemistry existed between them. Tamsin Olivier told me, 'It is perfectly true that my father never got along with, or spoke well of, Joan Fontaine, although he believed the film to be an important landmark in his career. He did admire Daphne du Maurier's work.'

Others of the cast also insulted Joan, though behind her back. 'Gladys Cooper was talking one day,' Joan told me, 'and I overheard her say, "That Fontaine girl – she is American. I don't think she can act."'

Judith Anderson, who was convincing as the black-garbed, sinister housekeeper, Mrs Danvers, was someone else who felt insecure on the set, still nervous and ill-at-ease with the mechanics of the cinema. She recalls that at times Joan wanted her to be menacing, to help her get into her characterization. 'There was one scene in *Rebecca* that Joan had to undertake which involved shedding real tears;

glycerine tears wouldn't do. Suddenly, without warning, she said, "Slap my face!" Being new to motion pictures, I was shocked. "What do you mean, slap your face?" I asked her, and I told her I wouldn't do it. To my amazement she went over to Hitchcock, who wasn't too pleased at her trying to make such an arrangement. Joan said to him, "Slap my face," and he let out a great big smack. Whereupon Joan sat down and humped her little shoulders, and out came the tears.'

Fortunately, Selznick was pleased with the rushes and Joan's performance. Throughout the making of the film, he insisted that Hitchcock follow the script very closely, and that meant retaining many of du Maurier's ideas and her narrative. Hitchcock understood the book and his film had many of the same undercurrents, including Mrs Danvers' unhealthy interest in Rebecca, though the sexual content of the film is reported to have worried Selznick. What for instance, would audiences understand Jack Favell and Rebecca to have been doing in the boathouse? What did Rebecca tell Maxim that he could never reveal 'to another living soul'?

The scene that particularly illustrates these darker connotations takes place in Rebecca's bedroom. Judith Anderson, as Mrs Danvers, had to open various wardrobe doors and – with more than a hint of eroticism – run her hand over Rebecca's furs, gowns and underwear as she further humiliated the new young bride. Judith was unable to manage this scene, saying that she felt Mrs Danvers should actually see Rebecca.

Hitchcock declared that he would act out the scene for her. He opened the closets and caressed the rich chinchilla coat; in a fraction of a second he became not only Mrs Danvers, but Rebecca as well. The portly Hitchcock's camp playing of this scene reduced both Judith and Joan to hilarious laughter, but as captured on film the sight of Mrs Danvers brushing the furs against the side of Joan Fontaine's face is enough to induce a feeling of unease in audiences even now. (Though it was not discussed publicly at the time, both actresses fully understood the implications of the scene, as Joan Fontaine made clear in her conversations with me years later. Discussed publicly, or made more overt, it would have led to problems with censorship in America, and further cuts would have been made to the film.)

Joan Fontaine and Hitchcock developed a good working relationship, so good in fact that he would use her in his next film, *Suspicion*, for which she would win the Oscar for 'best actress' of 1941 (many people thought she was awarded this because of not getting it for *Rebecca*). Hitchcock had storyboarded *Rebecca* in great detail, with the cameraman George Barnes and the art director. Joan knew what he wanted from her, and this helped her to develop the character of I de Winter.

For many years Hitchcock told a story that David Selznick wanted to end the picture with Manderley burning, and the smoke rising from the building to form a huge R in the sky. Luckily this was changed, and the film ends with a close-up of an R in a piece of embroidery in Rebecca's bedroom.

Selznick watched the final set of rushes. 'I am disappointed in the lighting in Rebecca's bedroom – we should make it more interesting – and we are a little slow in getting to the embroidered R. Otherise I think it's fine.' Audiences have agreed with him now for half a century – *Rebecca* plunges them down a mist-strewn drive and into over two hours of narrative cinema at its best.

The audience know the house is a model, that Fontaine and Olivier are not really on the French Riviera, and that the

Cornish cliffs are Californian. But the film retains all the rococo Englishness that made the novel so attractive. It is Hitchcock at his most masterly, and it stands as a supreme example of his craft.

With a score by Franz Waxman, *Rebecca* contained all the qualities of the original novel. Although Daphne du Maurier had not been able to visit the set and see what was being done to her book, the news she heard from her long-standing friend, Gladys Cooper, was encouraging. Years later, Daphne told me, 'I was surprised with the treatment of *Rebecca*. I had worried that the film would turn out like *Jamaica Inn*, but I was proved wrong. The film was perfect, and I wrote to Selznick and Hitchcock and told them so!'

All the cast had turned in good performances. Olivier was compelling as the haunted Maxim, Joan Fontaine perfect as the mousy heroine, George Sanders suavely sinister as Rebecca's cousin Jack Favell, Reginald Denny fine and upstanding as Frank Crawley, Gladys Cooper (who wrote later that Fontaine bore a marked resemblance to du Maurier) was impeccable as Maxim's sister, while Judith Anderson was ominous and rather threatening as Mrs Danvers and Florence Bates fascinating as the vulgar Mrs Van Hopper.

The film won an Oscar for 'best film', and there was an Oscar nomination for Joan Fontaine. When it was released in March 1940 it had exceeded its original budget of a million dollars, costing 1.28 million dollars, but eventually it would gross 2.5 million dollars during its release.

Following the success of the film, Daphne du Maurier was asked to adapt *Rebecca* for the London stage. This she did with some trepidation. She told me: 'Although my Daddy was an actor, I have no real interest in the theatre. In fact, it rather embarrassed me.' But she finished the adaptation, and found that casting was again to be a problem.

Sir John Gielgud remembers: 'I met Daphne for the first time around 1940, at Binkie Beaumont's office. They wanted me to recreate the Olivier role of Maxim de Winter on the stage. I considered their proposals, but decided to decline the offer. I returned to the Old Vic to do something more classical. I regretted this decision later, because the play was a great success and ran for many months.'

It was Owen Nares who finally took on the role of de Winter, while Celia Johnson played his mousy second wife and Margaret Rutherford Mrs Danvers. What brought about the closure of the stage version of *Rebecca* was the war. The London Blitz was in full force, and the Strand Theatre was bombed and destroyed. Among its ashes was found a small statue of Gerald du Maurier, which was returned to Daphne; she had given it to the cast as a good luck token.

As she grew older, Daphne became puzzled by the success of this, her most famous novel, which she always referred to as 'my *Rebecca*'. Although she didn't normally re-read her own work, so many people asked her about it that she had to go back to it from time to time. By the 1980s she thought the story to be rather old-fashioned. When a reviewer called the book 'romantic', however, she was quick to jump in and defend it. '*Rebecca* isn't romantic,' she told me. 'It is a study in jealousy and murder, not romantic at all.'

In the late 1970s BBC Television asked Hugh Whitemore to dramatize *Rebecca* as a serial, to be directed by Simon Langton. The production starred Joanna David as the second wife, Jeremy Brett as Maxim de Winter, and Anna Massey as Mrs Danvers. It was filmed in actual Cornish locations, with Caerhayes Castle being used as the fictional Manderley — Daphne thought this choice wrong, as it bore no resemblance to her idea of Manderley. However, the television serial did follow the book closely, though it was remarkably different from the Hitchcock film.

Joanna David too found that there was more to Daphne du Maurier than she had originally thought. 'Anna Massey and I did discuss the almost lesbian interest the housekeeper had in Rebecca and the young girl, and we tried to play our parts with some conviction.'

After the television serial, Opera North commissioned an opera based on the novel. 'I thought them foolish to attempt an opera,' was Daphne's reaction. 'I could never quite imagine my novel working to any degree of success as an opera.' In fact, the opera composed by Wilfred Josephs was well received (Gilly Sullivan sang the role of Rebecca), and was broadcast on Radio 3. In December 1987, five years after its first performance, it was revived, again being conducted by David Lloyd-Jones, the artistic director of Opera North until summer 1980. Perhaps it, too, like the film and the stage version, will be seen again and again.

Fifty years on, *Rebecca* remains a beautifully crafted and highly evocative novel. In 1980 Daphne published *The Rebecca Notebook and Other Memories*, the last book she worked on herself. But again, in that she told the public only what she wanted them to know. None of the private feelings that had made her write *Rebecca* in the first place were revealed.

Rebecca still evokes a vanished dream of England with descriptions such as: 'Tea on the lawn with the sound of the sea coming up from the shore, birds singing at dawn and rooks circling round the trees.' But Daphne du Maurier was to get nearer this dream than most when she became the tenant of Menabilly hard by Fowey, as they say in Cornwall.

5

The Lady of Manderley

'Menabilly was a colony to itself … The gardens
were extensive, surrounded by high walls, and laid
out to the eastward on rising ground, which, when
the summit was reached, looked down over dense
woodland across to further hills and the highway
that ran down to Fowey, three miles distant.'

The King's General

After the publication of *Rebecca*, Daphne found – to her
great disbelief – that she was one of the most popular and
celebrated authors of the day. The novel had captured the
imagination of the world, and after the film was shown in
1940 the many accolades it received meant that film
companies were going to be interested in all her future work.

Part of *Rebecca*'s popularity was due to its being seen as
representing something that was threatened by the German
invasion: the English way of life. Even though it was
produced in Hollywood, in the United States, an escapist

film such as *Rebecca* boosted British public morale and, in Winston Churchill's words, achieved 'more for the war effort than a legion of seasoned troops'.

The dedication page of her next well-known Cornish novel bears the dates 'January–June, 1941'. The title had been used, years before, by Sir Arthur Quiller-Couch, but he gave his consent to her using it again for her new novel. *Frenchman's Creek* was both a romantic and escapist story, and owes its genesis to a real place. The Helford River and its surrounding countryside are difficult to find, and many people believe that Frenchman's Creek does not really exist – it is perhaps one of the most remote and elusive landscapes in the du Maurier canon.

This remoteness has helped to protect it from commercialism's worst excesses, and it is little changed since the time when Daphne du Maurier first visited the area around the village of Helford during her honeymoon, in 1932. It was, she said, 'completely captivating; never had I experienced such a tranquil setting'. Local people, though, are cautious about entering the creek, many of them believing that it is haunted by the past and malevolent spirits. Part of its spooky reputation arises from the misfortune of an old man who, taking a short cut across the creek, did not return home one night. In the morning his body was found sitting upright in the river, his hat still on his head, his long white beard trailing into the water, and locals say that his spirit still appears in the houses and cottages he knew in his lifetime.

Frenchman's Creek is set in the seventeenth century, and Daphne learned from her study of Cornish local history that French sailors and pirates often visited Cornwall then, carrying contraband and alcohol for their Cornish friends. She makes the hero of her tale a French pirate who is making daring raids on the Cornish coastline, and who hides his vessel, *La Mouette*, in a pool of the creek which is shrouded by trees and hidden from the open river. The heroine, Dona, Lady St Columb, has wearied of her London life, and fled to Cornwall to 'avoid people, to be alone'. While the landed gentry try to capture the Frenchman, she finds excitement and passion by conducting an adventurous love affair with him, living 'the lovely folly of that lost midsummer which first made the creek a refuge, and a symbol of escape'.

This is Daphne at her Cornish best again; like *Rebecca* it has a haunting opening that conjures up vivid pictures of Helford River country. Always a writer with a strong sense of location, she describes the east wind blowing up the the river and its shining waters becoming troubled and disturbed – as does the life of the beautiful Dona.

Though the book contains many references to a Philip Rashleigh, who lives down at Fowey (and in one exciting adventure Dona and the Frenchman make a raid on Fowey harbour, where they capture Rashleigh's boat and sail it out to sea), when Daphne talked to me about *Frenchman's Creek*, she told me that the story on the whole was imaginary. 'The house, Navron, was based on one of the old houses on the Helford River where I had enjoyed a cream tea.'

Published in 1941, this book – 'the closest I have come to writing a really romantic novel' – was a success, the reviewer in the *Sunday Times* rather pompously predicting that the story's heroine was 'bound to make thousands of friends, in spite of her somewhat questionable behaviour'. Quiller-Couch's prophecy had been correct. That *Frenchman's Creek* is still well-loved, read and enjoyed all over the world, proves that it – like *Rebecca* – has stood the test of time.

Like *Jamaica Inn*, it has passed into the folklore of the

area, and in 1989 the Ferryboat Inn in Helford village was revealed as the centre of a twentieth-century smuggling ring, concentrating on the importation of drugs such as marijuana and cocaine. I had told Daphne several years earlier about the criminal goings-on in the area, but she had declared: 'I'm not interested in the little people who get caught, but in those who really run it, the ring. Now, if I were to set a drugs ring in an old Cornish house, then perhaps we'd have the start of another novel.'

The film rights of *Frenchman's Creek* were sold to Paramount Pictures for £30,000 shortly after publication. Joan Fontaine was cast as Dona St Columb, with the Mexican Arturo de Cordova as the romantic lead, the pirate Frenchman; Basil Rathbone and Reginald Denny were also in the cast. Joan Fontaine had not originally wanted to do the film; she was under contract to David Selznick, and by the terms of that contract was paid 1,200 dollars a week. However, Selznick was proposing to loan her out to Paramount for 2,500 dollars a week. He had already loaned her to Fox; since making *Rebecca* she had appeared in *Suspicion*, *This Above All*, *The Constant Nymph* and in the title role of *Jane Eyre*. She felt it was unfair that Selznick, who had benefited greatly from her performance in *Rebecca*, should be profiting from her in this way.

In addition, the director, Mitchell Leisen, was not someone she took pleasure in working with. He had directed her sister, Olivia de Havilland whom he admired, in *Hold Back the Dawn*, but Joan knew that he regarded her as being much less talented and felt that he favoured her sister. However, after much persuasion, she agreed to make the film, telling Leisen, 'I'm going to give you 1,200 dollars-worth of work a week, and that's all!' Then she laughed, and they all relaxed.

Leisen, Joan reflected to me, 'was the wrong director for the job. He wasn't interested in directing *me* at all. Mitch Leisen and Billy Daniels, the director of photography, were far more interested in the sailors who played the pirates! During the filming, Mitch spent an enormous amount of time arranging one of the sailor's – his boyfriend's – earrings.'

Leisen, whom Carole Lombard described as 'one of my closest girlfriends', was known for the many romantic films he made, and for the strong performances he could elicit from actresses he liked. His films had a visual lustre and entertaining pace, but on this occasion his flamboyant and over-the-top direction detracted from some aspects of the story and made it seem rather camp.

Frenchman's Creek was to be filmed in Technicolor, and Leisen was determined that the film should indeed be colourful. When the designer of the extravagant costumes, Raoul Pene du Bois, showed Joan the bright red wig and garish pink dress it was proposed she should wear in this, her first colour film, her composure vanished. She walked out. Her husband Brian Aherne intervened, and a few weeks later she was shown more appealing costumes, and eventually agreed to continue with the film

Filming took place in northern California, beyond San Francisco, at a place called Fort Bragg; in some ways it is rather similar to the area around the Helford river in Cornwall. Joan told me: 'We couldn't film in Cornwall at the time because of the war, so we went to the north of California, to Fort Bragg, where there are inlets covered with trees and ferns which grow down to the water's edge. Actually, it looks a lot like Cornwall. In some ways I hated the film because Charles Boyer, my favourite leading man, was not playing the pirate. Arturo de Cordova, who was

Mexican, and a lot shorter than me – and I am not very tall –
was not a convincing French pirate! I was not generally
pleased with the results of the film.'

Joan may not have been happy with her performance, but
Daphne du Maurier enjoyed the film. It was another
box-office success. 'My husband loved the film,' she recalled,
'and it became a favourite of his, because so much of the
music used on the soundtrack was taken from Claude
Debussy's "Clair de lune".' Years later, when Daphne
broadcast on Roy Plomley's long-running radio programme
'Desert Island Discs', she chose this music as one of the eight
records she would want if she were cast away on a desert
island.

After she had completed the novel of *Frenchman's Creek*,
and while she was living at Hythe, in Kent, Daphne had
heard from her sister, Angela, that there was to be a sale at
Menabilly. 'Everything is to be sold up, and the house just
left to fall to bits. Do you want anything?' What Daphne
really wanted was the house, and everything in it – but she
knew this was a dream. It was wartime; who knew if there
was a future for anyone? And Menabilly was entailed, so that
it could not be sold; her dream must die.

It is perhaps significant that her next novel, *Hungry Hill*,
was set not in Cornwall though still in a real location –
Hungry Hill is a mountain behind the town of Glengariff in
County Cork. Daphne wrote it when she was pregnant with
her only son, Christian (Kits) and renting a house in
Cornwall; the history of south-west Ireland, and of Dunloy
Castle where part of the story is set, was told her by an Irish
friend living in Fowey.

This gave her ideas for her plot, which concerned itself
with two feuding Irish families over several generations. The

Donovans are dispossessed of Hungry Hill, and see the Brodricks sink a successful copper mine there. Two hundred years later the Brodricks, Wild Johnnie and his mother Fanny Rosa, close the mine. Johnnie is killed by an angry mob, and his mother, who is sympathetic to the miners, reopens the mine (thus ending the feud) but dies of typhoid contracted from the Donovans. Published in 1943, *Hungry Hill* sold well.

However, 1943 found Daphne in Cornwall and, fifteen years after she had discovered it, she revisited Menabilly for the first time since the war began. Saddened and angered at the way the house was being left to decay, on an impulse she telephoned her lawyer and asked him to write to the owner of Menabilly and ask him to let the house to her. To her surprise, a week later she learned that she would be able to rent the place. Her husband was serving overseas, but she made up her mind. She would take it.

When she first mooted the idea of moving into Menabilly, her friends thought she was quite mad, so neglected and run down had the house become. Parts of it were quite beyond repair. But the success of her books, *Rebecca* in particular, had made her a wealthy woman and after a few months the ivy was removed, the roof repaired, the windows mended, electricity and the telephone installed, the plumbing attended to.

It seems that Tommy, as she always called her husband, was rather worried at the rash way his wife had signed the lease. A charming and dashing man, in some ways he protected her from the outside world and he was not at first in favour of their having a house so far away from London as their permanent residence. But when he arrived from Tunis for leave that Christmas he found a fire in the grate, a hot bath waiting, the furniture arranged just as he liked it and sprays of holly behind every picture. 'Well, I must confess, I didn't know you had it in you,' he told her.

Her furniture looked right in the panelled library and in the elegant white-walled drawing-room, large rooms with long windows overlooking the lawns. Philip Streatfeild's full-length portrait of her father, Gerald, stood high above the wide oak staircase, together with a large portrait of herself and her sisters.

Daphne had brought the old building back from the dead with her capable overseeing of workmen and cleaners, acting more like an army sergeant than a distinguished lady novelist. However, local people grew used to seeing this famous writer wearing men's trousers and one of her husband's old caps, and considered her merely eccentric. Tommy, too, seems to have accepted her penchant for male attire, though her dislike of social gatherings and 'the pleasant drink in the officers' mess' did annoy him. All army wives are expected to attend such functions, but to Daphne this meant dressing up and she hated it; she would even refuse to accompany her husband to Buckingham Palace.

In order to accomplish what had to be done at Menabilly she had assumed a military air of determination, and her obsession with the house lasted the twenty-six years she lived there. A large summer house was placed at the bottom of Menabilly's gardens, from where she could enjoy the view of Polridmouth Bay and the Gribbin Head, and it was there that she wrote. It is no exaggeration to say that this house and its grounds were to be Daphne's great love affair, second only to the affection she felt for her husband – though she was in many ways the least conventional army wife imaginable. Her father and grandfather had led rather unconventional lives, and she enjoyed knowing this, as she had enjoyed her own Bohemian past. But she appreciated her new position as lady of the manor, and would do nothing to spoil it. Her life in Menabilly echoed the life of the heroine of Rebecca as it should have been, another example of something she had created in her imagination becoming part of her real life.

By 1943 she had three children – Tessa, Flavia and little Christian – and in her own words became both their mother and their father. When she moved into Menabilly there was a nanny to look after the children, and later she engaged Miss Waddell, previously her own governess, to look after them.

Tommy became Lieutenant-General Frederick Browning in January 1944 and was, not unnaturally, fully occupied with the war. He was given the command of the newly created 1st Airborne Corps (composed of 1st and 6th Airborne divisions and the Special Air Service brigade) and in June found himself supervising 6th Airborne's landing on the left flank of the invasion of Normandy. The commander of the ground forces was Field Marshal Montgomery, who was a great admirer of Daphne's writings. He used to send her fan letters from the desert or battlefields in Europe written on the backs of cards, old wrapping paper, anything he could lay his hands on. 'He loved my books, you know,' she told me, 'and often asked me how I had imagined this and that. Oh! It was of great amusement to me.'

This unusual friendship did not go unnoticed and many years later Ken Follett wrote a spy novel, *The Key to Rebecca*, set in the desert war, featuring Montgomery, and using Daphne's novel as the basis for a spy code. There was some basis of truth to this, and Daphne lent me the book: 'Read it, dear, and let me know what you think.'

In early September 1944 Montgomery – and Eisenhower – realized that the Germans might be able to stop the Allied advance along the River Rhine. They would, after all, be defending their fatherland and Hitler had assured the German people that not one metre of their land would be invaded. Operation 'Market Garden' was designed by Montgomery to secure bridges so that Allied armies could advance north, and Tommy took a leading part in the planning of it. The northernmost bridge was that at Arnhem in Holland, which was to be seized in a surprise attack by airborne troops.

'I think we may be going a bridge too far,' said Browning, prophetically.

On 17 September the largest airborne operation in history set forth on its ill-fated flight. Taking part was the British 1st Airborne Division, 2,800 transport planes, 1,600 gliders. The venture, hastily organized, at first seemed to be efficiently executed. But on 18 September bad weather hampered flights bringing in reinforcements and supplies. Browning, who must take much of the blame because he was in charge overall, had failed to foresee such a hazard. He and his intelligence body had not done their homework, and a great many men were dropped into an area where a crack German Panzer division was undergoing manoeuvres. Signals were inadequate, because the Arnhem troops lacked equipment powerful enough to communicate over a distance greater than three miles. The remnant of the division, about a quarter of its original strength, was withdrawn on 25-6 September, and the operation is now remembered mainly for the unnecessary loss of life.

Browning's character was not strong enough to resist Montgomery, and he had allowed himself to be steamrollered into accepting an operation about which he had misgivings. He was a good and loyal officer, but he was not a brilliant tactical soldier; and the disaster at Arnhem greatly affected him for the rest of his life.

His second in command was John Dutton Frost, who held

the bridge with his troops against tremendous odds. Now Major-General Frost, he remembered further: 'General Browning was remiss because he did not make sure there were sufficient back-up teams. There was no radio contact, and air support did not exist. I do feel he was responsible.' This incident of the war in Europe continued to haunt Browning until his death, and his widow for even longer.

After the disaster of the Arnhem landings, Browning was sent overseas to be chief of staff to Mountbatten, who had specifically asked for him and thought him 'a man of very high principles, immense courage ... most loyal'. Their headquarters were in Ceylon, and after the Japanese surrendered in August 1945 there was the best part of a year to be spent in Singapore – for long months Daphne and Tommy were again separated. His career kept him abroad until 1946, when he was withdrawn to London, to the post of military secretary to the secretary of state for war.

During that time his wife was at her adored Menabilly, working in what Sheila Bush, her editor for many years, referred to as 'a hut at the end of the garden'. Daphne did a lot of her own typing, resulting in many mistakes. Sheila Bush told me: 'For thirty-five years it was my task to edit Daphne du Maurier's books, fiction and non-fiction, beginning with *The King's General* in 1946 and ending with *The Rebecca Notebook* in 1981. There was quite a lot of work to do on the finished typescript. I would have it retyped before returning it to her. Many people believed Daphne wrote with one eye on the *Saturday Evening Post* and the other on Twentieth Century-Fox, tailoring her stories to suit popular demand. This was not the case. She wrote, and could only write, at the bidding of her extraordinary imagination.'

The gestation of Daphne's novels followed a very definite pattern. She once told my Cornish publisher, Michael Williams, 'I have to think about it for months ... nothing on paper, just thoughts. Then I do a draft of notes, a skeleton, if you like. I go through each chapter, and then I re-read the book as a whole.' The actual writing seems usually to have taken six or seven months.

Her first novel to be written at Menabilly, one set firmly in Cornwall, was *The King's General*; the idea for it came when she read some historical papers connected with the Rashleigh family. For Daphne an old tale or a local superstition was enough to set her imagination afire, and at about the same time she happened to read the memoirs, mostly about the English Civil War, of the Royalist Honor Harris, written shortly before her death in 1653.

Combining these with the papers generously given her by the Rashleighs, she was able to put real events from the Civil War into the compelling story she wove. Her husband was away fighting, she had time on her hands, and Menabilly and the surrounding countryside were a perfect setting for *The King's General*. Her worries for Tommy's safety helped her to re-create the feelings of anxiety which had gripped people in south-east Cornwall as the early stages of the Civil War raged there. The ravages of war and its deprivations in the seventeenth century were being paralleled in twentieth-century Europe as she wrote. It took her less time than usual, only three months of so of actual writing, and was published in 1946.

This book, too, uses real Cornish locations – Pendennis Castle at the mouth of the River Fal, Launceston Castle, the Dodman and the Gribbin head – to great effect, and its pages are peopled with members of the great Cornish families such as the Arundells of Trerice, the Trelawnys of Trelawne and Sir

Charles Trevanion of Caerhayes.

The King's General novel is a brilliant re-creation of the love shared by Sir Richard Grenville (the King's general in the West), and Honor Harris, as courageous as she was beautiful, at a time when Cornwall echoed to battle cries as men decided whether they were for King or Parliament. But it is more than a love story, for Daphne's sense of history and her personal knowledge and insight into the county enabled her to resurrect seventeenth-century Cornwall. In one chapter she writes of the area she had claimed as her own, the narrow piece of land between Fowey and Par, where the Parliamentary forces, under the Earl of Essex, fought a hopeless battle at Castle Dor.

An intriguing sidelight on the story of *The King's General* is that, in 1824, Sir William Rashleigh of Menabilly was having various alterations made to the house and in the process masons discovered a small room, or cell. Seated on a stool, dressed in the clothes of a Royalist cavalier, was the skeleton of a young man. On consulting the family archives, Sir William discovered that members of the Grenville family had hidden at Menabilly before the abortive Royalist rising of 1648, and therefore surmised that one unfortunate gentleman had taken refuge in that secret room – and had been forgotten.

Daphne's vivid imagination led her to believe that something more sinister had happened to the man, and that he had been murdered. Publicly, she said many times that she had never seen a ghost; but in private she would confide that the young cavalier stood beside the large fireplace in the drawing-room at Menabilly and smiled at her. She told people that nothing remained of the seventeenth-century house that Sir Richard Grenville would have known, but in fact the Long Gallery survived as the drawing-room.

While Daphne wrote this first novel to be composed in their new home, her thoughts were often with her absent husband, and the dedication of *The King's General* read 'To my husband, also a General, but, I trust, a more discreet one!'. This caused a rift between them. Daphne's marriage had never been the most conventional of alliances, and a few family friends said that Browning had married Daphne on the rebound. He had had several affairs before their marriage, and this perturbed and worried her.

She admitted to me, on many occasions, that there had been other women during their marriage, one of them a friend extremely close to her. 'Does it matter?' I asked her once. 'It was you he married.' She paused a long time before answering. 'Yes, it matters,' she replied quietly, and never mentioned it again. Browning's indiscretions had obviously affected her deeply.

He took exception to the wording of the dedication, and tried to have it removed, thinking that Daphne was hinting at the failure of the Arnhem operation and the long period he had spent with Mountbatten in Ceylon. It was known in upper-class circles that Mountbatten was a joyous bisexual, who had enjoyed many affairs with members of his own sex. Daphne, too, was fully aware of his special idiosyncrasies. Her almost 'mannish' attitude to life, with the scant regard she paid to clothes and make-up, caused some people to wonder about her sexual orientation also.

Throughout this time there were constant rumours that the Brownings' marriage was in difficulties. Daphne hardly ever joined her husband in the officers' mess, and she remained – or tried to – far from public view in an isolated large house in Cornwall. However, as Major-General Frost points out, 'This often happens with serving soldiers, who are stationed away for several months at a time.' Many people believed that Browning had mistresses while he was stationed in London, and for a time – because of the physical distance between them and the length of time they had been separated – theirs was a marriage in name only. It would take some years before Daphne would again feel close to her husband.

She had found her father Gerald overbearing at times, and her mother, Muriel, lacking in affection for her; because of this I believe that her passionate nature was often suppressed and she found it very difficult to show physical affection. During this period she herself appears to have had no meaningful relationships with other men, although she had close friendships with several women, including Gertrude Lawrence.

After the war ended, and Tommy was able to be at Menabilly more often, Daphne and he picked up the threads of their marriage. In 1948 he resigned from the army, and was appointed to the office of comptroller of the household of the newly married Princess Elizabeth, an appointment that came from Lord Mountbatten's recommendation.

After Browning's royal appointment, a London base had to be organized, and a flat in Swan Court, Chelsea, was obtained. Daphne (who had not yet acquired a driving licence) would go up to London on the train, wearing her Town clothes. Her former housekeeper, Violet Hooper, remembers: 'Lady Browning usually wore a costume (a matching tailored jacket and skirt) when she went up to London, which she loathed. It was nothing too startling, nice but quite plain. She always had a taxi to the station, and then she caught the night sleeper to London.'

At the end of the war Mountbatten would often visit Daphne and Tommy in Fowey and stay with them at Menabilly for short periods of time. I was told that he used to enjoy strolling casually about the narrow streets until people took to applauding when he appeared. The people of Fowey recognized him as a war hero, but their appreciation made him more cautious about showing himself in public.

It is perhaps not widely known that Daphne entertained, stayed with and based some of the characters in her plays and novels on members of the Royal Family. Indeed, Daphne told me that she had based the character of Evan Davies in *September Tide* on Prince Philip, who stayed at Menabilly on two occasions at the invitation of her husband. Tommy Dunn, who farmed at Menabilly Barton for many years and was a neighbour of Daphne's remembered: 'Just after my wife and I were married, we were told that Prince Philip was staying at Menabilly. The Prince was seen walking across the lawns of the house with the General and Daphne, making their way down to Pridmouth Bay.'

While he was stationed abroad, Tommy Browning had acquired a sixty-foot fishing vessel, a tramp steamer which he sailed back from Singapore and renamed *Fanny-Rosa* after the character in *Hungry Hill*; he kept her in Fowey Harbour. Ron Bennett, the town's ship's chandler, recalled: 'Around 1948 the General, as I knew Browning, came into my shop. He was fitting out his boat, *Fanny-Rosa*, for a trip, and evidently the Prince was to accompany him. During those years my father had a little office in the shop, and on the wall of his office was a picture of an old seaman, sitting on the toilet, with his trousers down, saying, "Close the door!". Browning asked my father if he could borrow the picture to place in the toilet of the *Fanny-Rosa*. Browning enjoyed a joke, and said this picture would really amuse the Duke.'

Tommy Browning was responsible for encouraging both the Prince and the Queen to enjoy many quiet corners in the

Daphne greeting Gertrude Lawrence on her arrival in England to play Stella Martin in the West End production of *September Tide*. Daphne had created the part with Gertie in mind.

Standing outside what she called her 'hut at the bottom of the garden'. It was here at Menabilly that Daphne wrote the majority of her work. (*Camera Press*)

The film of Daphne's play *The Years Between* starred Valerie Hobson alongside the celebrated actor Michael Redgrave. This film has never been shown on television. (*By courtesy of Valerie Hobson*)

Daphne and her children Kits, Tessa and Flavia walking up from Pridmouth Bay. This photograph was a special favourite of Daphne's which she kept in her bedroom. (*Popperfoto*)

Daphne, dressed rather eccentrically in an eighteenth-century army uniform which belonged to her husband. (*Popperfoto*)

The Browning family pictured outside Menabilly in 1950. (*Camera Press*)

The 1953 film of *My Cousin Rachel* starred Richard Burton and Olivia de Havilland. (*By courtesy of Sally Burton*)

Vivien Leigh, Laurence Olivier and Daphne arriving at The Boltons, the Kensington home of Douglas Fairbanks Jnr. (*Popperfoto*)

Hitchcock's film of 'The Birds' – although different from Daphne's original story – was well made and well received.

Daphne and Tommy relaxing at Menabilly. (*Popperfoto*)

environs of Fowey and Par, and the Prince was heard to say that he very much appreciated 'getting away from it all'. A keen sailor, Prince Philip decided that it would be a good idea to keep a boat ready and waiting for his excursions around the waterways of Fowey. *Bluebottle* was stationed over at Polruan, on the far side of the harbour, and locals got used to seeing Prince Philip sailing round the harbour on quiet afternoons with General Browning, commodore of the Royal Fowey Yacht Club at the time, and accorded quasi-royal status himself through his illustrious connections.

When Princess Elizabeth became Queen in 1952, Browning moved to Buckingham Palace as treasurer and comptroller to the Duke of Edinburgh. Daphne disliked social gatherings, being uneasy out of her own environment. Though she was reluctant to attend, Tommy expected her to be there at functions held at Buckingham Palace, Balmoral and Sandringham.

In 1953 or early 1954, Daphne accompanied her husband to Balmoral and, once there, occupied herself by trying to work on her next novel, *Mary Anne*. It was a wet afternoon and the Queen sat looking out of the window at the Scottish rain, lightly rapping her fingers along the sill. In those days she was not at ease making light conversation, and it was the Queen Mother who asked Daphne what she was writing. (It seems that she, and other members of the Royal Family, were fans of Daphne's, intrigued and fascinated by her novels.)

'I am writing about my great-great-grandmother, Mary Anne Clarke. She was mistress of George III's second son – Frederick, Duke of York, the Prince Regent's brother,' replied Daphne. The Queen Mother, once Duchess of York herself, smiled, and with a twinkle in her eye told her: 'Well, dear, you want to write about it *all*. Don't miss anything out.'

Menabilly was a big house, and Daphne had live-in staff to help keep it running. She received an enormous amount of mail, and Browning's secretary, an Indian girl, would come down to Menabilly from time to time and help with this. During the 1940s Gladys Hooper and her step-sister Violet were trusted and discreet servants, and before them there had been Mrs Hanks. Gladys remembered seeing Prince Philip there: 'He was very quiet and did not really speak to me. I think he slept in the blue guest-room. He and the General went out sailing together.

Despite the brief spells she had to spend in London, Daphne was only truly happy at Menabilly. She cherished her home and her lifestyle, even though she spent many hours alone without her husband, who only visited occasionally at weekends. At Menabilly she could wear what she liked, and organize her days as she wished – she enjoyed living her dreams as much as dreaming them. Her life was kept ordered and private by her staff.

Violet Hooper (now Mrs Lemin) told me something of her routine: Daphne's day would begin at about nine, with breakfast in bed, then around ten o'clock she would have a bath; after this she attempted to write until lunchtime. Lunch was served at one, and Daphne liked simple good food without too much flavouring. 'Her favourite was lobster salad, or Dover sole with lemon – she was very easy to please.' Even if she was alone, she always took her meals at the dining table. After lunch she would go for a walk with one or two of a succession of West Highland terriers, across the fields and cliffs to the beach; in the evenings she invariably changed into a long housecoat or evening trousers, and generally wrote for another couple of hours.

Daphne hardly ever wore a skirt at Menabilly, but nearly always soft cord trousers with a jumper or shirt. While she was writing part of *The King's General* she took to wearing a gold-braided eighteenth-century military uniform belonging to her husband. Violet Hooper, who described it as being 'a lovely red colour with gold braid and buttons, about three-quarter length and fastened with a belt' told me that, 'Lady Browning usually wore this during the day. In some way it gave her inspiration to write, especially from a man's point of view.' Bryan Forbes, whom she met when he was playing Jimmy Martyn in *September Time* saw her wearing it when he visited her at Menabilly later and thought it 'rather fun and a little eccentric'.

Bryan Forbes stayed with Daphne at Menabilly on two occasions. 'I remember one time I returned to holiday in Cornwall, to visit people I had been evacuated to during the war, in the village of Helston. On this occasion Daphne told me that she rented Menabilly on a month's lease, and that the owners could make her leave with just a few weeks' notice. Part of the house was not used at all. I also remember that during my stay Menabilly was full of the sound of bees, very like an H E Bates novel. The whole estate was captivating. I also adored the many paintings of Daphne and her family that graced the walls of the house.'

Violet also remembers other visitors to Menabilly, including both Gladys Cooper and Gertrude Lawrence, who usually came for long weekends. 'Miss Lawrence and Lady Browning wrote each other at least a couple of times a week. When she arrived at Menabilly, I noticed how wonderfully dressed she was. Miss Lawrence was so slim and very attractive. She and Lady Browning would put on trousers, and would go out for long walks together, along the coastline. During these visits I often served lobster salads. I remember that Miss Lawrence usually visited Lady Browning when the General was in London. I don't think there was anything unusual about their relationship, but they were extremely close friends and I could tell that Lady Browning was extremely fond of her.'

Violet also recalled the tremendous affection Daphne and her husband showed each other, particularly if they had been separated for long periods of time. 'It was always "Ducks" this or "Darling" that, they adored each other.'

When Daphne was invited to take part in local activities she always refused. 'She wasn't rude, she just didn't want to get involved,' Violet explained. 'Her life was writing her books. We never disturbed her when she was writing in her hut at the bottom of the garden.' However, she was friendly with a least one person who lived locally, Miss Halliday from Carlyon Bay, recalled by Violet as being 'a very tall and handsome woman in her cord trousers' who often stayed with Daphne and cooked her meals.

Even with the large amounts of money her work was earning her, Daphne clung to her simple country life; deductions for tax didn't frustrate her as they might have done anyone who wanted to lead a different lifestyle. 'I sometimes think how fantastic it is that, in spite of all I am paid, I couldn't live much more elaborately than I do here at Menabilly. I don't suppose my father made anything like it!' She also confided to me that being the larger earner in the household had caused its own difficulties. Tommy's army pay had in no way approached what she earned through her writing, and he was uneasy about accepting extra money, which he regarded as 'handouts'.

Daphne's three children were growing up, and she wanted to give them something of the enchantment of her own childhood. She was a very good mother, and people noticed that her children were always referring to her or talking about 'Mummy'. Their grandmother, Lady du Maurier, often stayed at Menabilly, for after she was widowed she and Daphne seem to have grown closer. She would drive herself there, accompanied by her little Pekinese dogs, and according to Violet, 'She was not a fussy woman although, unlike Lady Browning, she wore a lot of make-up.'

Until they were twelve, Tessa, Flavia and Christian were taught at home by their mother's former governess, Miss Waddell, whom they too called Tod. On many summer afternoons Daphne would amble down to Pridmouth beach with all the children, and a large basket containing a picnic prepared by Violet to be eaten on the beach. Holidaymakers could hardly believe that the lady dealing out the sandwiches, orangeade and tea from a flask was Daphne du Maurier, author of *Rebecca*.

Translated into twenty languages, this was the work that had really made her famous. The French version of the film had been stored in a vault in Paris during the war and, fortunately, survived: the French première was on 22 May 1947. Hollywood had paid her £10,000 for the film rights: a lot of money at the time, though the film has since been seen by millions of people, and its distribution must have earned thousands, if not millions, of pounds or dollars more for those who controlled it.

Of the £30,000 she was paid for the film rights of *Frenchman's Creek*, income tax deductions left her with £3,000. The film rights of *The King's General* were bought for £65,000, one of the highest sums paid for a novel at that time, in 1947. Sir Alexander Korda had intended to produce it, and after Daphne had finished writing it had sent a crew down to Cornwall to film the author at work at Menabilly. He was forced to abandon the project when it became clear that he and his studio had overstretched their resources.

Stewart Granger told me that he had expected to star, with James Mason, in the film of *The King's General*. 'I was asked to portray the character of Sir Richard Grenville, and I looked forward to playing someone straight out of the pages of history. Sadly, the film fell through; I landed an MGM contract in Hollywood so I left England, with my wife, Jean Simmons, for the USA.' James Mason told me that he, too, left for the larger studios of Hollywood, adding that he and Granger did eventually work together, in 1952, when they made *The Prisoner of Zenda*, in which Granger played Rudolf Rassendyll/King Rudolf V to his Rupert of Hentzau.

Only really happy at Menabilly, Daphne disliked being away from Cornwall for any length of time – but in 1947 she made her first visit to the United States. The reason for this was that she had to appear for the defence in a suit for plagiarism brought against Selznick International by the family of an obscure writer who said that the story of *Rebecca* was taken from a novel called *Blind Windows*. Daphne took her two youngest children (Tessa was at boarding school), and they stayed with her American publishers, Nelson and Ellen Doubleday, who became 'the dearest of friends'.

Fortunately, Daphne's method of working – producing a skeleton outline and notes for each chapter – was already established when she wrote *Rebecca*, and she still had the notebook in which she had made her preliminary jottings in Alexandria ten years earlier. This notebook was produced in court and, after cross-questioning, the judge dismissed the case. (The notebook was given to Ellen Doubleday as a memento, and returned by her daughter to Daphne after Ellen's death; it is included with other writings in *The Rebecca Notebook*.)

The case had been dismissed but it had shaken Daphne, though she claimed to remember little about either it or that first trip to the States (apart from being seasick all the way home in the *Queen Mary*). One of the most famous and successful writers in the world, with her books available almost everywhere and selling by the million in a score of languages, still she did not think she was 'a really good writer'. She could not face literary parties, but she longed for praise from the serious 'high-brow' critics who dismissed her work as 'just romantic'.

Her life at Menabilly, the house she was obsessed with for so many years and in whose wild wooded grounds sweeping down to the sea she had trespassed before she even dared to dream that one day she would live there, was like an enchanted story. She wanted the magic never to end. The ancient grey house in the hollow above the sea was remote, but with her loyal staff and her little dogs for company she was more than content there.

'I think people were envious of me working at Menabilly, though they used to ask me if it wasn't a bit too far out, if I wasn't lonely there,' recalls Violet Lemin. 'But Lady Browning was one of the kindest people I have ever worked for.'

Daphne admitted to me that she thought it strange 'to love a building so much'. When she took up residence in 1943, though parts of it were derelict and would later have to be demolished, it was already filled with history, a history to which her years there added. While she was chatelaine it saw distinguished visitors: Lord Mountbatten, Field Marshal Montgomery, Prince Philip and the Queen.

Only once did she panic. In 1962 the Queen and Prince Philip paid a royal visit to Fowey, which they would leave on the royal yacht, *Britannia*. They were to visit Menabilly in the afternoon, and Tommy Dunn remembers that he and many others gathered outside the gates of Menabilly to see the Queen drive by. She stayed with the Brownings for about an hour, and Daphne had ordered a lavish tea-time spread from Fortnum and Mason in London, complete with brandy snaps filled with cream. Alas, the Queen does not eat in the afternoon, so none of the food was touched!

Ron Bennett's wife still laughs at the memory of 'eating the Queen's left-overs' at Angela du Maurier's house, Ferryside.

6

The Versatile du Maurier

'I looked up and saw my name in lights, and the
title of the current film, *Rebecca*. There were lines
of people standing in a queue, waiting to go in. I
did not join them.'   *The Rebecca Notebook*

The past is an abandoned stage whose players are dead and
nearly forgotten. All that we have kept across the years are
echoes and images, some giving a true likeness, others – like
a poor camera – filtering the truth through layers of
imaginings. The du Maurier tradition of theatricality was
strong in Daphne, but in her it took a different turn. Despite
being the most attractive of Gerald du Maurier's three
daughters, she never had any desire to follow her father on
to the stage.

Exposed at an early age to well-known personalities of
stage and screen, she did not particularly admire them or
enjoy their company. She would rather draw or read a book
than talk to many of them, though she formed lasting

friendships with two of his leading ladies: Gladys Cooper (on whom Daphne would base the character of Mad in her last novel, *Rule Britannia*) and Gertrude Lawrence.

Daphne told me that she thought Gladys was probably the only woman in the world who never flattered Gerald, giving him instead a genuine platonic friendship throughout his career. Gladys never allowed herself to become one of 'the stable', as his daughters rather indelicately termed his little gallery of favourites. When J M Barrie's *Peter Pan* was first performed, she played the title role, with Angela du Maurier as Wendy and Gerald as a blood-curdling Captain Hook.

'I enjoyed watching my father act,' Daphne recalled. 'I thought him wonderful, but the theatre didn't appeal to me personally. In fact, when we went backstage after a show, and people came round with their congratulations, I found it all most embarrassing.'

Gerald once said that Gertrude Lawrence was his favourite leading lady, both on stage and on screen; they made a film, *Lord Camber's Ladies*, together at Elstree in 1932. Now best remembered for her professional partnership with Noël Coward and her performances in his comedies and in musicals, Gertie was an international star in her own right. This was at a time when stardom meant exotic furs, diamonds, first-class trips to New York and the South of France. Surprisingly, in Gertie's company, Daphne seems to have revelled in this kind of lifestyle.

They probably first met around 1932, when Gerald and Gertie appeared together in John Van Druten's *Behold We Live*, and she became a frequent visitor to Cannon Hall in Hampstead. Eleven years or so older than Daphne, in many ways Gertie was an unlikely friend for her – nevertheless their friendship was a close and intimate one, perhaps rather similar to that Daphne shared with Fernande Yvon.

Gertie was a complicated, volatile and explosive character, who had many changes of mood. Annie Leon, who appeared with her in *September Tide*, remembers that sometimes she 'would swear like a lorry driver, but on other occasions she behaved like a sweet angel'. Daphne had never had a close relationship with her mother, and it may have been that which she sought; even so, many of their friends thought that Gertie's interest in Daphne was unhealthy. They were inseparable. Daphne appeared to adore Gertie, following her about, sitting and listening to her, loving every moment in her company.

When Daphne herself broke into theatrical headlines, it was with the forthright and honest biography she wrote of her father. Knighted in 1922, Sir Gerald du Maurier was widely regarded as being at the head of his profession when he died in 1934, and Daphne's biography of him (published the same year) caused fellow members of his club, the Garrick, to flinch and mutter, 'I'm jolly glad my daughter can't write.'

He had changed the general attitude to acting in the early part of the twentieth century, bringing a natural, easy air to the parts he played. The first actor to light a cigarette on stage, the first to wear his own street clothes, the first actor in fact to look much the same on the streets of Piccadilly as he did across the footlights, he was a brilliant man, full of idiosyncrasies – perhaps rather like Peter Sellers. He would speak with many different silly voices, attempt stupid pranks, play practical jokes. He was entertaining as a companion, but hell to live with. Daphne was his favourite daughter, but his fierce possessiveness denied her freedom both during his lifetime and later, for it undoubtedly had an effect on her ability to feel and express emotions.

She remained fond and proud of him, however, and stood

up bravely for her work. 'Father always said, "You have got to tell the truth," and I wrote the book as he would have written it – at least, that's how I see it,' she said in an interview she gave when *Gerald* was published.

Later on, several of her novels, including *Frenchman's Creek, The King's General* and *My Cousin Rachel* would be adapted by others for theatrical presentation, but she also wrote three plays for the theatre herself.

There would be *September Tide* in 1948, but first there was the adaptation of *Rebecca* in 1940, which was bombed out during the war, then a play called *The Years Between* in 1945. Set in the Second World War, it features an MP, who is reported killed in action, and whose wife, Diana, is persuaded to stand for his constituency, which she wins. Diana is on the point of remarrying when her husband returns from a POW camp to find a budding independent career woman instead of the wife he had left; if he wishes to keep her, he must accept the changes. (Is there perhaps an echo of Daphne's own life here? While her husband was away she had become successful and wealthy, taken on Menabilly ...)

The Years Between was staged at Wyndham's Theatre in London and had a long and successful run starring Clive Brook and Nora Swinburne. Faith Brook remembered the play: 'It was a real return to the stage for my father, after his many years making films in Hollywood. He received tremendous applause when he first walked on stage, but I don't think he gave one of his most convincing performances.'

Nora Swinburne, aged 87, also remembered: 'Daphne du Maurier visited the play during its pre-London run at Brighton. She did not stay at the large hotel on the front, but around the corner in a small and less impressive hotel. She was small in stature and not a showy personality at all. I found her to be charming, and rather retiring. The play was a great success, and I think we ran for nine months.'

The film rights were sold to Rank in 1946, and it was announced that Michael Redgrave and Valerie Hobson would star in it. Daphne declined the opportunity to write the screenplay because she was too busy writing a novel (*The King's General*) and the screenplay to her previous work, *Hungry Hill*.

The screenplay for *The Years Between* was written by Sidney and Muriel Box. Muriel Box, though in her seventies, remembered: 'Daphne du Maurier never got involved with the film at all, she refused to be consulted over the script. Sidney was rather furious that one scene from the film was used in another picture, *The Captive Heart*. It is the moment when Michael Redgrave returns from the war to see the iron gates missing and he is told that they have gone to help the war effort.'

Valerie Hobson also had memories of the film. 'I enjoyed the part of Diana very much, especially my scenes at the House of Commons, which had been re-created at great expense at the studio. Redgrave and I got along wonderfully well, and the film was produced at the Riverside Studios, near Redgrave's new home. I remember meeting Daphne at least a couple of times, and she appeared to keep a benevolent eye on the whole proceedings. I don't think this film has ever been shown on television ... Daphne du Maurier's work was quintessentially English, and Hollywood was lucky to have the opportunity of using her stories.'

Daphne had not been involved in the film adaptations of *Jamaica Inn* or *Rebecca*, and the screenplay for *Hungry Hill* was the first she had attempted to write. She was assisted by Francis Crowdy and Terence Young (later to become famous as the director of the James Bond films *Dr No* and *From Russia With Love*, as well as *The Amorous Adventures of Moll. Flanders*).

Terence Young told me how he had changed the screenplay of *Hungry Hill* 'because Daphne's original draft darted all over the place. So I just rearranged the text and added some extra dialogue. I feel the film did not do the book justice. I remember having lunch with Daphne at the studio and she told me how she had enjoyed one of my previous films, *Dangerous Moonlight*. She also hoped that the music in *Hungry Hill* would be as good as the Warsaw Concerto!'

The film, which was begun in 1946, had a large budget; in its cast were two newcomers: Michael Dennison, and Pete Murray (who would later abandon acting to become a disc jockey). Pete recalled the film with great affection when he spoke to me about it. 'Never a good rider, I had to ride my horse to the top of the model of Hungry Hill which had been created in the studio. It refused to go up the hill. I was playing a cavalry officer, but my horse had to be led up the hill by an extra – to a few rude remarks from the crew!' He also recalled that he and Jean Simmons had to go to a theatre in Golders Green to learn how to dance for the film. 'It was interesting, as I couldn't dance well at all.'

Michael Dennison told me that he, too, had had trouble with his horse. 'Margaret Lockwood, Dennis Price and I had to ride out in one scene, and I remember having to do several takes, because my horse kept walking in front of Margaret Lockwood's – she was supposed to ride out first, past the camera.'

Daphne found that the film was not particularly well received, and she was disappointed that her efforts did not help it reach a wider market in the UK and the United

States, regretting her involvement with the making of it. Very seldom shown on television, it is one of the least-known of the films of her work. When I showed her some stills from it she commented, thoughtfully, 'The photos look better than the actual film turned out.'

Throughout her adolescence and early adulthood, Daphne seems to have been drawn to strong-minded women – even after her marriage to Tommy in 1932. She allowed few people to see the sexual side of her personality, but in actuality she was sophisticated and brittle and rather charming and captivating. There seems little doubt that as a girl she was highly sexed. She had one lover, Carol Reed, before she married; that it was only one does not make her the innocent abroad she would have had people believe.

In later life this aspect of her personality seems to have been sublimated, changed into an obsession not for any person but for a place – Menabilly. Here it was that Gertrude Lawrence (whom she described to me as 'a truly wonderful girl') came to spend weekends when Tommy wasn't there; she reminded Daphne of the past, and of the wonderful years when Gerald was king of the London stage and a world celebrity.

In the late 1940s, when Daphne was writing her third play, *September Tide*, she realized that the character of Stella would be ideal for the now middle-aged Gertie. The story of this play was based on something that had happened to Daphne, though so disguised that not many people realized there was an autobiographical element. It revolves around a self-centred artist who has married a young girl; she will, he believes, clean his paint-brushes and not bother him. The play is set in Cornwall, in the Falmouth area, where the artist has been dragged on a duty visit to his mother-in-law – whom he falls in love with. She, too, is swept away by passion but recovers her senses and sends the young couple off to America to make a fresh start.

Daphne sent the script to the States, to Gertie and her husband, the producer Richard Aldrich, expressing the hope that they would find it suitable for production on Broadway. They read the play and were in agreement that it would not be successful in America, it was too English. 'But,' said Gertie, 'the part of the mother, Stella, is a role I could do something with. I could play it, and I could make a success of it – in London.'

It is easy to see why the part of Stella Martyn appealed to Gertie: it was a rather glamorous part, playing an enchanting and susceptible woman, and it would make a fitting farewell to her London admirers. The cast assembled was a distinguished one: as well as Gertie herself, it co-starred Michael Gough as artist Evan Davies, while Annie Leon appeared as his wife, Cherry Davies, the young Bryan Forbes as Jimmy Martyn, and Dandy Nichols as Mrs Tucket, the daily woman. Costumes for the leading lady were designed by Edward Molyneux; smart and simple, they were completely in character with Stella.

The director was Irene Henschel, who was married to Ivor Brown, drama critic of the *Observer*. According to Annie Leon, 'Irene was a dithery old dear, and she could not control Gertie at all. Gertie said one day, "To think I have come thousands of miles to act out this piece of shit!" Nevertheless the play progressed well, and Daphne and her husband kept a watchful eye on the proceedings. *September Tide* opened its pre-London tour with a week's run in Oxford. 'Terrific social event,' reported Gertie, 'printed invitations To Meet Miss

Gertrude Lawrence!'

The play went to Blackpool, Leeds, Liverpool and Manchester. Binkie Beaumont of H M Tennent, who had undertaken the production, was thrilled by its success. It had broken all box office records in the provinces and taken over £3,000. Daphne, too, who had visited the play many times on its out-of-town run, was delighted.

Four days before its opening at the Aldwych, the joyous expectancy surrounding Gertie on this, her first appearance in London since before the war, was already evident. Wherever she went, she was greeted with enormous affection by people of all ages and classes, and she responded with humility and grace. She was in a fever of excitement about the approaching London opening, and wrote to her husband:

> Darling Germy,
>
> I am worried about your cold, be a good boy. Daphne, Tommy and Mo [Lady du Maurier] are thrilled that you are coming. Don't bog it up, ducks. Such a night will never happen again, and you must be there. It would be an empty night for me if you were not there.
>
> Am very excited
> Much love
> Mrs A

The opening of *September Tide* on 15 December 1948 at the Aldwych Theatre has gone down in London theatre history as the first gala first night since the Second World War ended. The pre-war feeling of glamour and excitement was infectious: men had taken their white ties and tails out of storage, and women were dressed in dazzling new creations designed by London's leading fashion houses. Queues of devoted theatre-goers waited patiently for hours – indeed, many had queued all night – in the chill and cold of the evening.

Inside the theatre, Gertie had been given two dressing-rooms and both were filled with flowers. The group of her admirers, headed by Lou Hollis, who called themselves the 'Orchid Club' had sent her a large mauve orchid. But pride of place on her dressing-table went to a single red rose from Daphne, with a simple message: 'Gertie, all my love, always, Daphne.' She was superstitious about any gift from Daphne; its arrival confirmed that she was still loved.

The royal box had been dusted and regilded for the occasion. Lady du Maurier was there with Tommy, now an officer of the royal household, and on her left sat Richard Aldrich, who had conquered his germs sufficiently to join them.

The play was a personal success for Gertie, sweeping her back to the forefront of the public's love and attention, and making news. It brought to the war-wearied Londoners, financially and politically worried, not a reminder of happier days but hope that they would return to the kind of world they had known. A large crowd gathered to wait outside the star's dressing-rooms, and outside the stage door.

Everyone agreed that Gertie was a triumph in the play. It did not worry Daphne particularly that her contribution went unsung because it was Gertie's night, but she had hoped for respect – if not admiration – from the critics. Their view of the play drew a sharp line between its merits and Gertrude's performance. Critic W A Darlington wrote in the *New York Times*:

When Miss Lawrence takes the stage, we find that …

inevitably she transcendentalizes the part. Everyone agreed that the occasion was a triumph for Miss Lawrence ... For Miss du Maurier hardly a good word was said. All the same, she will have a smash hit on her hands.

He was right; the play was a success, drawing even royalty to the Aldwych. In *Mrs A*, the biography he wrote of Gertie after her death in 1952, Richard Aldrich quotes from her letters:

> They fight with umbrellas to get into the matinees, as though we had announced nylons going free ... Binkie sends me flowers for breaking records ... HRH The Duke of Edinburgh was in the front the other night and came back afterwards, he and Daphne are old friends ... We are hoping their Majesties will come ... Queen Mary has returned from Sandringham and she usually comes to the plays first, and then the Reigning Monarch.

Because of Tommy's connection with the royal house-hold, both Princess Elizabeth and Princess Margaret came to see the play, as did Queen Mary (bringing with her her own portable toilet; she never used anyone's private facilities). During the interval the whole cast was introduced to her. Michael Gough recalled:

'Out walked Queen Mary and made a regal progress until eventually she was standing in front of Gertie who curtsied from her chin to the floor. Queen Mary said to Gertie, "The only person I can't hear is you. Please speak up!" Gertie mentioned that they had met before, when she was acting in a play with Sir Gerald du Maurier. Queen Mary haughtily replied, "I don't remember. It was a long time ago."'

The Queen's coldness was due to the fact that Gertie had once had an affair with the Prince of Wales (before Mrs Simpson came on the scene); the mother of the man who should have been King of England could not forgive this indiscretion. Unknown to her many fans, Gertie had many sexual relationships – with both men and women, though it has to be said she was most attracted to the former.

After Queen Mary had left, the humiliated Gertie broke down in tears. No one noticed that the interval was extended a little longer than was necessary for the cast to be presented to the Queen, and, after a delay, she was back on stage.

Daphne went to see the play many times: 'Daphne was like an aunt visiting her nieces and nephews, or that is I what I felt,' said Michael Gough. 'She was very attractive, and quite the charming lady, fascinated by the theatrical tradition in her family.' He asked her how she created her characters. 'I am like a postman,' she told him. 'I think of myself delivering a letter when I am writing. Most of my characters are based on real people – only sometimes are they invented out of thin air.'

Many of her fellow actors were afraid of Gertie: legends had grown up about her, and she could be imperious and forbidding. Bryan Forbes, who was on the threshold of his career, remembered an incident from *September Tide*.

'I was very excited about appearing in Daphne's *September Tide*, and I also admired Gertrude Lawrence. I found Daphne to be a charming and kind person – in fact, during the run of the play, she took me, along with her husband and children, to Battersea Funfair to enjoy the rides. Her husband, who'd been in charge of 1st Airborne Corps, was sick! Anyway, Gertie and I had to sing a song at the end of the play (we'd chosen a tune that was out of copyright). On one occasion, because my voice was not very good and I was inexperienced, Gertie lost her temper and stormed off, saying, "That boy will have to go!"

'I left the theatre very downhearted and returned to my unimpressive digs. Later in the evening I received a phone call – it was Gertie saying she was sorry, and asking if I'd like to join her for breakfast. I think I had my first oysters on that occasion. I was reinstated in the play.

'Daphne remained friendly with me after the play; she even wrote a charming little note for my first book, which greatly pleased me. She was so kind.'

'As much as I admired Gertie,' Michael Gough told me, 'her bouts of temper were sometimes difficult to deal with, especially for a young actor like me. I remember that one day a door had jammed on stage; Gertie's next change was down to her bra and knickers, and she did it at the back of the stage. As soon as she spotted the assistant stage manager, she yelled at him, "F—— off, you shit!" Just because the door had jammed! She could be angelic one minute and quite awful the next. I had never heard an actress use such language. I was fully aware of the impact that Gertie's friendship had on Daphne – she was devoted to and besotted by her. Every day during the run of the play there would be a small bouquet of flowers for her from Daphne in Cornwall. During the play Gertie got away with blue murder, and Daphne was so smitten she just smiled.'

Richard Aldrich commented on Gertie's friendship with Daphne: 'I am sure that she was frequently bewildered by the rapidity and mutability of her own impulses, possessed as she was of an intuitive rather than analytical intelligence ... I doubt that she really understood herself clearly any more than did most of those who thought they knew her intimately. An exception in this regard was Daphne du Maurier.'

When *September Tide*'s West End run was over after 267 performances, Daphne went with Gertie and Richard Aldrich to New York for a holiday. She seems to have enjoyed the break from Tommy and the children, and to have gone sightseeing happily with Gertie. It was on this holiday that she talked to Aldrich about his wife, telling him all about her 'moodiness and variability ...and sense of vague self dissatisfaction'. Not surprisingly, he was amazed at the personal and intimate knowledge she had of Gertrude's private feelings.

Daphne hoped to write something else for Gertie to appear in, and her novel *Mary Anne* bears the sad dedication:

> To Mary Anne Clarke my great-great-grandmother
> died Boulogne, June 21st 1852
> and to Gertrude Lawrence
> who was to have acted the part on the stage
> died New York, September 6th 1952
>
> In memory of both

She also wrote a foreword to Richard Aldrich's *Mrs A*, something she very rarely agreed to do. (MGM took out an option on *Mary Anne*, it was rumoured as a vehicle for Elizabeth Taylor.)

During the 1950s Daphne had became less involved with the worlds of the cinema and the theatre, being caught up in – at least, to some extent – her husband's career as a courtier at Buckingham Palace. She hated the social gatherings this involved, and sometimes Tommy had to work very hard at ensuring she would attend them. The homesickness she felt in London often made her appear to be unhappy and ill-at-ease.

They still had the small flat in Swan Court, near Cheyne Walk and the banks of the Thames – it was little more than a *pied-à-terre*, but it served its purpose of providing them with a London base. Daphne told me that she would often walk beside the Thames, wishing she were back in her beloved Cornwall.

She was sometimes accompanied on her walks along the riverbank by Agatha Christie, with whom she had become friendly. Mary Fox confirmed this: 'I don't think, I know that Daphne was very friendly with Agatha Christie, and they swapped writing ideas. But she knew an awful lot of people for a so-called recluse!'

While Tommy was busy at the Palace, they would spend long hours in each other's company, often discussing plots and characters. (Daphne told me, later, 'I have always found Agatha Christie's books far too predictable; still, she knew how to tell a tale!')

Roy Moseley, the biographer, visited Daphne's flat at Swan Court: 'I remember finding Daphne fetching some milk in from the back door. She signed my copy of *Rebecca*, and she told me of her recent friendship with Agatha Christie. I found the idea of these two great story-tellers walking unnoticed together rather amusing.' In fact, Agatha Christie helped Daphne with *The Scapegoat*, and many of her plot ideas can be found there.

When Daphne was at home at Menabilly, she often went for walks down to the beach or along the headland. This would start her thoughts stirring, her imagination working, as she experienced Cornwall in its many moods, light and dark, summer and winter. Her love of and obsession with all things

Cornish led her to write her last truly Cornish historical novel, one which would again be turned into a memorable film – *My Cousin Rachel.*

Speaking to a Cornish magazine in 1963, Dame Daphne du Maurier said, 'Each book has given me pleasure but, you know, when it is completed the whole thing fades. Each has its phase. If you want to write about changes with the years, *My Cousin Rachel* possibly marked the end of a phase ... I cannot see myself sitting down to another Cornish novel.'

My Cousin Rachel did in fact turn out to be the end of an era: though she would write further novels, this was the last of her truly historical works set in Cornwall, and it marks an important chapter in her private story.

After the completion of the film based on it, she became still more reclusive, willing to see few people outside her immediate family, although she allowed a selected few friends the privilege of staying with her. Reluctantly, she was obliged to spend precious weeks in London, because of her husband's duties at Buckingham Palace; she felt out of place at the prestigious functions held there and only attended them when he persuaded her that her presence was absolutely necessary.

It was during the early 1950s that her light brown hair began to lose its colour, turning first grey and then white. Years later she told me, 'I have never tried to dye my hair, although it went grey very early. I felt I didn't need to, you know – I am not an actress.' She remained an attractive woman, however, and Michael Gough remembers her as 'being quite captivating'. 'If she set her cap in someone's direction, she would be quite difficult to refuse,' he said.

When *My Cousin Rachel* was first published in 1951 a reviewer for the magazine *Queen* referred to it as: 'dramatic, surprising and masterly; again, a highly skilled piece of story-telling.' Like *Rebecca*, it can be compared to Charlotte Brontë's *Jane Eyre* (or perhaps even to a Victorian melodrama). It is full of suspense, and ends in ultimate tragedy.

For many of Daphne's long-time readers, this novel is one of their favourites because it combines the vintage du Maurier ingredients of murder, mystery and poisoning. It opens with the memorable scene-setting sentence, 'They used to hang men at Four Turnings in the old days', and this strong sense of location continues throughout.

Ambrose Ashley marries the beautiful and mysterious Rachel, Countess Sangelletti, in Italy and never returns home. Over the following months his letters to his favourite cousin, Philip, hint that he is being poisoned. Philip therefore decides to travel to Italy, but he arrives too late – by the time he gets there, Ambrose is already dead. Shocked, and very worried, Philip returns home hastily to Cornwall. Then Rachel crosses the Channel, comes to Cornwall and stays at Philip's beautiful manor house. When Philip meets her he is attracted by her great beauty and her air of mystery, and as time goes by he finds himself torn between dark suspicion of Rachel and passionate love for her. Is she a scheming murderess, or is she the sweet and angelic woman she often seems? This perplexing doubt runs through the novel; did Rachel poison Ambrose, or didn't she? It is a question that is never properly answered, and it is left to the reader to come to a decision.

'Everyone asks me was Rachel guilty, or innocent,' Daphne often said. 'Do you know, I could never make up my own mind about that – actually, I think Rachel was the culprit. But I have always left my readers guessing.'

My Cousin Rachel again shows how Daphne combined

what she imagined with events that really occurred. Though she disliked leaving Menabilly for London, she greatly enjoyed travelling abroad. Florence provides some of the locations, and an Italian holiday in the early 1950s also influenced other parts of the story. 'The idea that Rachel poisoned Ambrose by using laburnum seeds in a tisane came to me when I was enjoying a cup of herbal tea. The lady who prepared it spent a considerable time on her choice of herbs, some of which could be poisonous if used in the wrong circumstances.'

Much of *My Cousin Rachel* was imagined at Menabilly: 'The idea of the sunken garden, which would cause Rachel's death, came to me one afternoon when I was out walking with my dog.' Once again, she used the estate and house she loved as the setting for her work, writing in the summer house at the end of the garden, and she based the name of the centuries-old Cornish family in whose house the story takes place to that of the owners of Menabilly, changing it from Rashleigh to Ashley.

She, or what she referred to as 'Eric Avon', her male *alter ego* (for much of the novel is told from a masculine point of view), drew on her imagination to create Philip Ashley, but Rachel was derived from a real character – Rachel Carew, whose portrait still hangs in the 'porch room' at Antony House in south-east Cornwall, a house still in Carew possession. Painted in the middle of the seventeenth century, the portrait had attracted Daphne's attention when she slept in that room during a visit – partly because its artist was a woman.

Mary Beale painted, among others, the physician Thomas Sydenham (known as 'the English Hippocrates') who took part in the Civil War on the Parliamentary side, the Royalist poet Abraham Cowley, and the Marquess of Halifax; she was a successful professional artist at a time when few women were able to pursue careers of their own. It should be said, though, that Rachel Carew was not in the least like her counterpart in the novel; the strongest similarities are that her husband's name was Ambrose (he was Ambrose Manaton of Kilworthy) and that she, like Daphne's heroine, died young.

The Four Turnings crossroads that appear at the beginning and end of the novel is a real place, not far from the end of the drive to Menabilly. Daphne's long hours spent researching the history of local families revealed that a gibbet had once stood at these crossroads, and that men were hung there for stealing and other crimes, their bodies being left dangling for days as a grisly warning to other possible miscreants.

Talking about *My Cousin Rachel*, Daphne told me that as she wrote it she imagined Vivien Leigh in the part of Rachel. 'Years ago, when I was in New York, Vivien asked me what I was writing, and I told her, "A book for you to star in!" Vivien would have been fine but, alas, something went wrong and Olivia de Havilland filmed the character.'

Hollywood had early realized that Daphne's books were likely to make good box-office and not many months after the book was published George Cukor (famous as a 'woman's director') came down to Cornwall to visit Daphne and to discuss the idea of filming her latest novel. Cukor could immediately see its possibilities, and the potential cinema audiences it would attract.

With Cukor came Greta Garbo. Many comebacks had been planned for her, but she had always turned them down. 'I have made enough faces,' she is reported to have said. Daphne remembered her as being 'tall, and rather masculine, but very charming with me – I don't know why.'

Unlike a lot of veteran actresses, Garbo had realized early on that, if she continued to work, she would have to compete with a younger version of herself. This, she told Daphne, she thought was 'so cruel, so harsh'. 'Why don't they treat me like any other actress?' she asked.

Because Garbo was still unsure about whether she wanted to undertake the role, a screen test was arranged; but she was unable to overcome her reluctance to appear in front of the cameras and the project with Cukor never even began. She did however say that if she had been planning to return to the screen, *My Cousin Rachel* would have been a more than suitable vehicle.

The film was eventually made under Henry Koster's sympathetic direction with Richard Burton playing Philip Ashley, opposite Joan Fontaine's older sister, Olivia de Havilland, as the infamous Rachel. When she read the script, written by her old friend Nunnally Johnson (who was also the producer on this picture), the teasing and maddening, but entertaining, melodrama set in nineteenth-century Cornwall with its 'did she/didn't she' mystery appealed to her. Never mind that she was following in her sister Joan's footsteps by appearing in a film adaptation of another du Maurier novel!

Richard Burton was excited at the idea of making his first American film and he enjoyed the fun of going to Los Angeles. Everything was one big adventure for him as he and his first wife, the Welsh actress Sybil Williams, were exposed to Hollywood. What chiefly pleased him was the enormous amount of money he was paid to act in *My Cousin Rachel*. Sally Burton, his widow, remembered that he used to say he went out 'with empty suitcases, and returned home with them full of food and presents'.

'As to the working relationship with Olivia de Havilland,'

she continued, 'one day Richard read a sign outside de Havilland's dressing-room which read "Olivia de Havilland must be referred to as MISS DE HAVILLAND, and not Olivia or Livvy, on the set of the picture".'

Though they got along reasonably well during their scenes together (they did not mix socially – she was an established star, while Burton was an inexperienced young actor, new to Hollywood) the grand attitude that she took did not please Richard Burton, and he brought a cold intensity to the love scenes, while she played them with appeal and sometimes great concentration. His performance was surly, but he proved a talented foil to the ambiguous, aggravating, ambivalent heroine whom she brought to the screen with an elusive, disconcerting personality, hard to pin down.

While he was making the film, which was mainly photographed at Twentieth Century-Fox in Hollywood, Henry Koster realized that the Cornish countryside could not be duplicated on the back lot in Hollywood. (He also realized how much better *Frenchman's Creek*, and even the excellent *Rebecca*, would have been if they had been filmed in Cornwall.) So a second film unit with Richard Burton and Audrey Dalton, who played the love interest, was sent to St Dennis, between St Austell and Newquay, in Cornwall, to film some exterior scenes. Daphne helped them by telling them which area on the north coast she had imagined the action of her novel taking place in.

Brook Williams (Emlyn Williams's son and Richard Burton's godson) told me: 'In order to film exterior scenes of horse-riding in the Cornish countryside, and the rolling crashing waves on the Cornish coastline, Richard went to Cornwall with Bluey Hill, the first assistant director, who had to make sure they did not shoot any telegraph poles or whatever.

'Richard was riding across a field, in full period costume and everything was going fine, when suddenly a farmer appeared out of nowhere shouting, "Git off my bloody land!" Richard told him that he was sorry, and that they were shooting a film. The farmer, getting more angry, replied, "I don't care what *you're* shooting," and fired his double-barrelled shotgun into the air. Richard's horse bolted, and off they went towards the horizon, with Bluey and the camera unit following behind. Though Richard was a reasonable rider, he could not control the horse. I wonder how many of the startled people who saw an unknown actor on a horse, completely out of control, charging through villages and across fields, ever realized later that it was the famous Richard Burton?'

The film of *My Cousin Rachel* did not reach a wide audience, though those who saw it enjoyed it. Richard Burton in particular had reason to be pleased with it: it brought him the first of the eight Oscar nominations he gained during his career.

The next book Daphne began work on was set in France, the home of her forebears, the Busson du Mauriers. They had owned a glass-blowing factory near the town of Le Mans, and there was also a family château nearby. Daphne's research led her to discover that the history of the family had not been half as grand as her grandfather and father had been led to believe, something which appealed to her wicked sense of fun.

She began writing *The Scapegoat* in 1956. Set in the present day, its story is that of a quiet Englishman, John Barratt, who is on holiday in France when he meets his double, Jean de Gué, an aristocrat who tricks him into assuming his identity. He then finds himself with a château, a crazy, morphine-addicted, bedridden mother, an unhappy wife, Françoise, and a teenage daughter. Barratt is trying to get to grips with the situation when the real Count returns. The real Count murders Françoise for her money, and tells Barratt to go. There is a duel, which Barratt wins. After all these interesting events, off he goes with the Count's mistress.

Daphne had always admired Alec Guinness, and enjoyed a great deal of his work, and she had written *The Scapegoat* with him in mind. So, at Binkie Beaumont's instructions, he turned up to meet her at Beaumont's office. Daphne was delighted to discover that they had a great deal in common, and a friendship grew up between them almost straight away.

Sir Alec Guinness, as he now is, lives in the country; like Daphne, he is not really a 'Town' person. Talking about his experience on the film of *The Scapegoat*, he told me:

'I was introduced to Daphne by Binkie Beaumont – it was he who said we should meet, and he sent me a pre-publication copy of *The Scapegoat*. We arranged to have lunch at a little restaurant in Gerrard Street (it no longer exists), and over lunch we found out we got along very well. We corresponded over the next few months. The film of *The Scapegoat* was eventually set up with MGM at Ealing under Sir Michael Balcon. Originally we had a lot of trouble with the script; Gore Vidal was the screenwriter, but he was not sympathetic to the story. It was I who suggested Robert Hamer as the director – he was someone I admired. He'd worked as an editor on *Jamaica Inn*, and he'd directed me in *Kind Hearts and Coronets*. He, too, worked on the script but because he was in the last throes of an alcoholic illness, he did not have much control over the whole proceedings.

'I rejoiced when I heard that Bette Davis was cast as my

mother, but we began with a misunderstanding. She thought the movie was one of her starring vehicles at Warner Brothers in the 1940s, and we got off on the wrong footing. She appeared to be very suspicious of me and Robert Hamer. I asked her out to dinner several times, but she never responded, and I sent her flowers – it would have been a much more enjoyable movie if we had got along better.

'She altered her costumes, and they became too elaborate, making her appear overdressed and affected. I think she should have worn an old cardigan, but she refused – this did not help the film. The sets and settings in which she played were dizzy with distractions – eye-catching bric-à-brac and rococo serendipity of every description. Although Davis behaved very correctly throughout filming, I am afraid she remained very distant.

'We filmed some of the movie on location in France, and Daphne told me she had imagined the story as taking place near Le Mans, where her ancestors had once owned a glass factory.'

The film, in which Irene Worth played the wife, Françoise, and Nicole Maurey the mistress, though very stylish, is an over-elaborate drama, and rather slow. Daphne was disappointed in the end product: 'Although I admired Alec immensely, and I wrote the novel with him in mind, he didn't give one of his best film performances. I was so convinced that he would be right, I formed a company with him to produce it. Before I had decided what to do about the film, I was offered Cary Grant to play the dual role. In hindsight, I think he *could* have been better at playing a modern man-about-town.'

Bette Davis, too, had strong reservations about it. In London in 1987 to promote her book, *This and That*, which told the world how she had recovered from a very serious

illness, she gave me an interview at the Grosvenor House
Hotel. 'The film of *The Scapegoat* did not do justice to
Daphne du Maurier's book,' she asserted. 'It was terrible, I
have never had such an awful working experience. You can
tell Daphne du Maurier I thought the film disastrous.' (It
was on this visit to London that the acerbic Miss Davis upset
the benign host of BBC television's chat show, 'Wogan', by
telling him, 'I am here because I am a saleswoman; I've come
to sell a book.')

Sir Alec told me that he had visited Daphne in Swan
Court: 'As I remember, it was a rather dreary flat. The
General, her husband, was very charming, he was a typical
gentlemanly figure. Daphne came down to my house in the
country to stay – she was very agreeable, and I was very fond
of her because we laughed a lot together. My wife, Merulla,
felt she was slightly resentful of other women.' ('I was very
young in those days,' explained Merulla, 'and Daphne rather
frightened me because she was so direct.')

'Even with a script by Gore Vidal, *The Scapegoat* did not
turn out as expected. This disappointed Daphne, and she no
longer felt any interest in getting involved with the filming of
her work. She and I owned a piece of the picture; I had a
twenty-five per cent share in lieu of a salary. It was released
in 1959, and a year or two later I gave Daphne back my
share; neither of us made a penny from this project. I think
the final editing, and the weak script, spoiled its chances of
success.

'After the film I saw Daphne on a few more occasions, and
we had a signed Christmas card from her every year. Then,
about 1980, we were going to Cornwall on holiday and I
wrote asking if we could meet again. Daphne refused, saying
she had not been well, and could not see anyone. I had
enjoyed her company, but I think that through her illness

she cut herself off from the majority of her old friends. At any rate, I took this unfriendly attitude as a rebuff, and a final farewell.'

7

Sinister Stories

Last night the other world came much too near
And with it fear.
'Another World', *The Rebecca Notebook*

Daphne du Maurier was not only famous as a novelist, she was also a prolific writer of short stories. The craft and technique of story-telling, particularly in shorter works where the idea and plot had to be developed quickly, interested her. She had been impressed with the composition and structure of Katherine Mansfield's short stories which she had read when she was just starting to write, and she had aimed at making her own work equally well written and convincing.

Throughout her life, Daphne objected to critics dismissing her work as 'just romantic', and would challenge interviewers: 'What about my short stories? They have murders and frightening themes, and deal with the supernatural.' 'The element of the macabre, which runs through many of my books, has – I think – grown stronger over the years, especially in my short stories,' she said to me once, during one of our many discussions of her work. Psychological drama and sinister elements came to the fore in these tales, which she regarded as illustrating her skill as a storyteller, and their treatment for the cinema by clever directors such as Alfred Hitchcock and Nicolas Roeg have certainly introduced her work to a new, and sometimes younger, group of readers.

In public Daphne would say that she had never seen a ghost (though in private she owned up to the cavalier near the fireplace at Menabilly), but her interest in supernatural topics was limitless. She had researched quite thoroughly, from books, the ways in which psychic phenomena occur (knowledge she used to great advantage in some of her short stories), and during the many months she was separated from her husband she had experimented with the occult. Mary Fox remembered, 'Daphne was always interested in spooks.'

Though she did not like people knowing that she was a psychic, she had a strongly developed sixth sense, and as a child had often known that something was about to happen before it did. Perhaps her writing career comes into that category: she was so confident of her ability that it was never questioned. She *would be* a writer; not might be, or would probably be, but *would be*!

During my early visits to her at Kilmarth, I was amazed at the depth of knowledge Daphne possessed about psychic matters. At the same time she was fascinated by poltergeists, noisy mischievous ghosts famous for their destructive powers. She was friendly with Colin Wilson, the writer on the occult; he told her about his experiences and she reported to me: 'Colin tells me he knows a man who can conjure up a poltergeist. What am I going to do with one of those? You know they only occur when an adolescent is reaching puberty, or around someone mentally disturbed.'

What she did with it, of course, was to put it in a story. She gave many of the characters in her short stories extraordinary powers and perceptions, but when it came to real confrontations with the spirit world and things unknown, her nerve left her. She might have been interested in the occult, but she did not want to be possessed by any supernatural power, whether malevolent or benign.

I had experimented with seances, and described to her the devastating effect that they had on me as an impressionable adolescent. I had developed a form of 'automatic writing', which would occur particularly when I tried to concentrate with an open mind, and it took years of self-discipline to make it leave me. Daphne agreed that to tamper with 'the unknown' can be dangerous, and told me that she had a similar experience when she was a girl. She and Angela had held a seance in the attic of Cannon Hall in Hampstead, an experience that frightened her but left her wanting to know more. By the time I knew her, it was an area of knowledge that disturbed her, particularly in the years when she was living alone at Menabilly and Kilmarth, both old houses with a haunted past.

Colin Wilson found her attitude exasperating. 'A psychic called Matthew Manning was staying with me in Cornwall, and he told me how much he wanted to meet Daphne. I rang her, and asked whether I could bring him over. "Oh no," she said, "that kind of thing absolutely terrifies me!" I tried to persuade her, telling her that Matthew was an extremely amiable man and that he certainly wouldn't materialize any ghosts, but she continued to say no. I must admit that I thought this was rather silly and neurotic, so after that I didn't contact her again for several years.'

Because of their film treatment, probably the most famous of Daphne's stories are 'The Birds' and 'Don't Look Now'. Many people do not associate 'The Birds' with her, even though the original story was set in Cornwall, but believe that Alfred Hitchcock, who directed and produced the film of the same name, made up the story himself. When he filmed it in 1963 he changed both the storyline and the location considerably, but it was based on something that happened to Daphne in the 1950s.

Living near the coast, as she did, she was accustomed to seabirds, and not frightened by them. Tommy Dunn, who farmed nearby, recalled seeing her walk through a flock of gulls on the ground without being in the least bothered by them. They looked at her, but she ignored them. However, she was staying at Menabilly for a welcome break from London, and walked down to the beach at Pridmouth one afternoon, closely followed by her devoted dog. As she reached the lake behind the beach, two large seagulls flew down and tried to bite the dog. At first she ignored what had happened and walked on, but then without warning the gulls flew straight into her face and she was forced to run into the trees for protection. (This strange behaviour, Daphne told me, was due to a shortage of food. When seagulls can't find food, hunger makes them do very unexpected things, and people who live near the coast are used to this phenomenon.)

This frightening incident, combined with what she observed one day when Tommy Dunn was ploughing, gave her the basis of the story. 'I got the idea for "The Birds" from watching the farmer plough the field behind the farm, at Menabilly Barton; the seagulls chased the tractor, flying down, apparently trying to attack the farmer. Coupled with my other experience, this gave me the idea of birds attacking humans.'

As originally published in the collection entitled *The Apple Tree* in 1952, 'The Birds' dealt with a farmer, Nat Hocken, and his family, who live in Cornwall. They are besieged in their farmhouse as millions of birds inexplicably start attacking them. The sheer strength of the birds destroys RAF planes, and the story ends bleakly, with Nat smoking his last cigarette, the radio silent, and the birds outside massing for their final attack.

Hitchcock bought the film rights to 'The Birds', but did nothing with them for several years. He was one of the few directors still working who had weathered the transition from silent movies to sound, but as the old-style studio-based Hollywood finally reached its tragic end in 1961 with *The Misfits* (the last film for both the King and Queen of Hollywood, Clark Gable and Marilyn Monroe), Hitchcock too seemed to be at a standstill.

Hollywood's stranglehold had been broken, and exciting and interesting new work from Europe had dramatically changed the nature of cinema. Directors such as Luchino Visconti, François Truffaut, Federico Fellini and Karel Reisz were establishing their reputations. For thirty-five years, when audiences had paid to see an Alfred Hitchcock film, they had known what they were going to get – and generally they had not been disappointed. But in 1961 there was no new Hitchcock movie, nor was there one in 1962; these were the first years without a Hitchcock film since 1925. *Psycho* was, he told friends, a hard act to follow; no film project interested him enough to start work.

He was looking for inspiration when he turned again to the writings of Daphne du Maurier. Like many directors, he used other people's ideas in the pursuit of his own career, and he never fully acknowledged the debt he owed her, even being scathing about *Rebecca* in interviews, calling it 'a cheap novelette'. But the psychological elements in this novel influenced the way in which the film of it was directed, admittedly at David Selznick's insistence; and in his later films Hitchcock appears to have built upon what he had learned and achieved in *Rebecca*.

While other directors feared television, Hitchcock had simply embraced it, establishing himself as master of another medium. He produced and hosted two mystery series for television, 'Alfred Hitchcock Presents' (1955-62) and 'The Alfred Hitchcock Hour' (1962-65). A mystery magazine and several book anthologies also used his name as part of their title (for instance, the 1967 volume was *Alfred Hitchcock Presents: Stories That Scared Even Me*), and he told François Truffaut that 'The Birds' was included in 'one of those *Alfred Hitchcock Presents* books'.

There had been unsuccessful attempts to dramatize the story on radio and television, but his interest in it was reawakened by reports of birds attacking houses and animals off the West Coast of America. As he said to Truffaut: 'Yes, these things do happen from time to time, and they are generally due to a bird disease, a form of rabies. But it would have been horrible to have put that in a picture, don't you think?' He was not worried about the enormous technical difficulties making such a movie posed: 'It's a job, let's get on with it. The basic appeal to me is that it had to do with ordinary birds.'

In Hitchcock's adaptation, the action takes place at San Francisco and Bodega Bay, California and the birds attack a whole community rather than just one family. The story had been altered, and the casting of the rewritten central character, Melanie Daniels, became of prime importance. Hitchcock's leading lady had been Grace Kelly, but in 1955, while she was working on his *To Catch a Thief*, she had met Prince Rainier of Monaco, and their marriage in 1956 meant she was lost to movies for ever. Hitchcock was still looking, without much success, for an actress to replace her. He and his wife Alma spotted a young actress, Tippi Hedren, doing a television commercial, and groomed her for stardom. Hitchcock shot extensive screen tests, and commissioned the famous Edith Head to design costumes for his new leading lady.

As rewritten, Melanie Daniels (played by Tippi Hedren) is fascinated by a young lawyer, Mitch Brenner (played by Rod Taylor), whom she meets in San Francisco and joins on a visit to his young sister at Bodega Bay. Early on in the film Melanie is seen with a bird cage containing a little bird; on their way across the Bay, she is attacked by a swooping gull, the first skirmish in the war about to be started by the local bird population. The gulls also attack Mitch's sister's birthday party, and a nearby farmer had his eyes gouged out by a crow.

Mitch and Melanie become trapped in the Brenner home, while the birds attack in legions, eventually breaking into an upstairs room and trapping Melanie. Rescued by Mitch, the family is driven away, and the film's final haunting image is all Armageddon, with the birds brooding and waiting as the car drives off into the distance.

Cinematically, this film posed a tantalizing problem: how to convey a world threatened by creatures generally regarded as benign. The first instance of their threatening behaviour seems to be random, but as the film develops the audience realizes that it is only the beginning, that something more terrible will follow. The birds gather for a more ambitious attack, and gradually hysteria builds up.

Hitchcock had wanted to end the film with an image of the Golden Gate Bridge covered in birds, but he abandoned this. There were many difficulties that had to be surmounted, and – though he was used to working to a very well-prepared script – in this film there was a great deal of improvisation in many famous scenes. The episode of the attack by the birds on the exterior of the house was done spontaneously, right there on the set.

'While we were shooting the movie at Bodega Bay,' Hitchcock recalled, 'there was an item in the San Francisco paper about crows attacking young lambs; this had happened in the same locality where we were filming. I met a farmer who told me how the crows swooped down to kill his young lambs. That's where I got the idea for the gouged-out eyes on the dead man.'

Tippi Hedren's memories of making the film were not all happy ones: 'I nearly went insane, because Hitchcock would not use doubles in some of the violent scenes with the birds. I spent several whole days trapped in a room, doing nothing except being attacked by specially trained birds.' On screen, of course, the effect was tremendous, but Hitchcock was accused of being unfeeling (to put it mildly), and Tippi was off the film for a whole week afterwards on account of the mental exhaustion which followed her ordeal.

The making of the film disturbed Hitchcock, too. Despite all the horror and suspense he evoked on screen, he was normally able to 'switch off' when he got home. But this film 'was getting to him' and he told Alma that he was 'tense and upset'. The nightmares were too real even for such a master of the macabre.

A sequence that Daphne herself thought was convincing was that set in the petrol station. An attendant is knocked down by a gull (Hitchcock explained that 'a live gull was thrown from a high platform, off-screen; it was trained to go from one place to another by flying just above the man's hand. He was an expert on movements, and overplayed his reaction, to give the impression that he'd been hit by the gull'); the nozzle he was holding falls to the ground and the gasoline flows; a motorist pauses without noticing this and throws down a lighted cigarette, causing an enormous explosion. During this sequence Melanie is trapped in a glass telephone booth, which recalls the earlier shot of the little bird in its cage.

This film is an excellent example of Hitchcock's best work, illustrating clearly his ability to shock and confuse his audience after lulling them into a false sense of security. (Watch it again, and – among other nice little touches – notice Hitchcock's famous walk-on scene at the beginning.) With over 1,400 shots, about twice as many as he usually used, 371 of them trick shots of one sort or another, it was one of his most expensive films. Throughout, certain vital elements remained deliberately fluid. It took Hitchcock a long time to settle on the right finishing shot, and – rather to his irritation – Universal superimposed a final 'The End' title so that audiences would not be left too disorientated.

In the publicity for the film, Hitchcock claimed, 'It could be the most terrifying motion picture I've ever made', but initial critical reaction was rather lukewarm. 'Great special effects,' commented the *New York Times*, 'stunning visuals, although the human characters are dull and colourless.' Nevertheless, the film was a definite commercial success, bringing even more fame to both Hitchcock and Daphne du Maurier.

The germ of the film is hers, while he depicts the way the world might end: not with nuclear explosion and a holocaust, but with the eerie cry of birds circling to the attack. The film's supreme technical achievements were not due to Hitchcock alone: he was very much helped by Lawrence Hampton's special effects, as well as by Ray Berwick's bird training, while Bernard Herrmann's electronic score was effective in heightening the tension and keeping taut nerves on edge.

Daphne was more than pleased with the results. She thought this was 'exceptional film-making, and I did not mind them changing the story this time, because the results were so convincing.' ('The Birds' was also liked by the more sensational of American film-makers, spawning a series of imitations in the 1960s and 1970s in which people were attacked by ants, rats, bees, and even giant rabbits!)

Although Daphne du Maurier has written many selections of short stories, many with supernatural and occult themes, none has grabbed the attention so successfully as 'Don't Look Now'. Throughout her career, she wrote about places rather than about people – and this particular story about supernatural or occult forces that led to a violent death in Venice conjured up wonderfully sinister visions of out-of-season Venice, that most mysterious of waterlocked Italian cities, with its canals, crumbling buildings and eerily deserted hotels full of shrouded furniture.

Daphne always preferred to stay in places out of season, so that she could absorb the atmosphere, and she used the insights she gained in her writing. Abroad, she was a different person, almost gregarious, and far more interested in eating out and socializing than she was at home. One of her holidays abroad was in Venice where she went with her son, and where she gained the background and ideas for 'Don't Look Now'. This story was published in 1971 in a collection entitled *Not After Midnight* in the UK, and *Don't Look Now* in the United States.

The book concerns a young couple, John and Laura Baxter, who have the misfortune to lose one of their two young children who dies of meningitis. In an attempt to overcome her grief, Laura accompanies John to Venice, where his work has taken him, and as they stroll through the city they catch glimpses of a small figure who looks from a distance just like their daughter. Laura has a series of encounters with two strange sisters, one of whom is blind and psychic. Laura's desire to believe that their daughter is still with them leads her to attend a seance, and she is told that the little girl has returned to warn of impending danger to her father. Laura is called back to England, but John sees her dressed in mourning, apparently going to the cemetery; a phone call to England establishes that she is safe. While she is away, John sees his daughter again, and pursues her through Venice, into a church; but it is not his daughter, it is a female dwarf, who murders him.

Various elements went into the writing of 'Don't Look Now'. At the time of Daphne and Kits' visit to Venice everyone was talking about a series of murders, committed by someone the newspapers described as a dwarf. Daphne got the idea of incorporating such a person into her story when she saw a small girl running by a canal. 'She turned her head, and revealed herself to be an evil-faced dwarf,' she told me. Daphne also happened to be passing a canal when the body of a woman was being taken out, and in St Mark's Square she saw elderly twin women. 'Right from childhood,' she told me, 'I have always enjoyed the challenge and discipline of constructing short stories, and they are generally based on some sort of personal experience. In "Don't Look Now", which is based in Venice, I saw the two old women, twins – one of whom was blind – sitting at a table in St Mark's Square, like some sinister sort of Greek chorus. In my story I gave the blind one psychic powers.'

Two years after the story first appeared in print, there was also a film version made by the brilliant director, Nicolas Roeg. Whenever the death knell sounds for the British film industry, someone appears whose work seems to offer a guarantee of its continued existence. In 1973, that person was Roeg. He has a photographer's eye for striking visual detail and was a distinguished cinematographer before becoming a director. He can juggle images with great skill to build up a complex pattern of associations, though in *Don't Look Now* his sophisticated approach is held in check by the limits imposed by du Maurier's story and the conventions of the horror thriller.

What attracted Roeg to Daphne du Maurier? 'Actually, it's rather a curious thing. As I read that short story, this premise never left my mind: "Nothing is what it seems in life." I thought this idea to be a wonderful disguise, and a great way to start a movie ... Daphne writes from inside the human condition; all her characters have depth, that is why she is a wonderful writer ... Also, the idea that nothing in life is what it seems sums up a lot of du Maurier's work, such as "The Birds" and *Rebecca* ... François Truffaut said to me, "Isn't it strange, Nick, we seem to make the same movie over and over again." This is why her work transfers so well to the screen, because it touches issues concerned with the human condition.'

This was what first attracted Roeg to this story, and this multiplicity of levels also strikes a chord within him. His film of *Don't Look Now* explores the theory that behind one door there is another, and behind that door ...

'When I did the recce for the film,' said Roeg, 'I felt that

Venice itself had some sinister qualities, and was not what it
seemed. It has been called the most beautiful prison in the
world, because you couldn't get away from it. In *Don't Look
Now* there is not one shot of St Mark's Square. I did not want
to fall into the trap that everyone seems to fall into when
photographing this famous city.'

It could be argued that Roeg outdoes Hitchcock both in
terms of dazzling visual style, and the creation of an
atmosphere of dread and foreboding. His first film as a
director was *Performance*, a vehicle for one of rock's most
unpredictable stars, Mick Jagger (and he would later direct
the controversial David Bowie); he brought Daphne du
Maurier's vision of out-of-season Venice, full of menace and
dread, to the cinema screen in a brilliant personal statement.

The film was cast with Julie Christie as Laura Baxter,
Donald Sutherland as John Baxter, and Hilary Mason as the
blind Heather. When Hilary Mason first visited Roeg at his
London office, she was able to tell him that she already knew
'Don't Look Now', having read it some time earlier; 'I told
him this and he took it as a good omen, because he is a very
superstitious man.' Julie Christie would have difficult scenes
to play as Laura, in which she would have to attend a seance,
and before filming started, Roeg took her to a famous
direct-voice medium so that she would have some
background knowledge.

From a casual opening showing a happy ordinary family,
the film develops into a ghostly mystery involving telepathic
powers. A series of repudiations and mistaken assumptions
run round in a circle to the dimly foreseen disaster. The first
shots are of the Baxters' pleasant rambling house in the
English countryside, just after Sunday lunch. Their two
children – a boy and a little girl wearing a red mackintosh –
are playing quietly in the garden. Nothing could be more

ordinary. John, who is a restorer of ecclesiastical artwork, picks up a slide he has recently taken of the interior of a Venetian church; as he examines it it becomes blotched with a bloodlike stain. Impelled by a mysterious premonition, he rushes into the garden – his daughter has fallen into a pond and disappeared beneath the surface. John dashes into the water after her, and seconds later is rocking her lifeless body in his arms.

The young couple go to Venice, leaving their son at his boarding school. Baxter is there to help restore Venetian churches, Laura to get over her grief. During their stay they meet two strange sisters, one (Heather, played by Hilary Mason) blind and psychic. Walking through the dark and brooding city of Venice, they catch glimpses of a small fleeing figure, clad in a red coat as their daughter had been when she was drowned.

The couple are trying to forget their tragedy, but Heather tells Laura she has seen the ghost of her daughter, and continues to describe her, and what she was wearing on the day she drowned. The child, she assures Laura, is very much with them. This news has a traumatic effect on Laura, who faints. When she is revived she feels a strange sense of elation that her little girl has not left her completely. John, on the other hand, is annoyed at the 'mumbo-jumbo' and refuses to have anything to do with Heather and her sister.

He cannot, however, dissuade Laura from attending a seance one night at the small *pension* where the two women live. While Laura is there, John spends the evening getting drunk and wandering up and down bleak alleyways in the city. The blind Heather, meanwhile, tells Laura that her daughter has returned to warn her father that his life is in danger, and that he must leave Venice immediately. John does not take the warning seriously, but a couple of days later, when he is working high up on a rafter of a church, matching some mosaics, he is overcome by vertigo. It is only by clutching at a dangling piece of rope that he saves himself from almost certain death.

Laura is called back to England because their son has had a slight accident at school. On the same morning that she has left John sees her dressed as a widow, standing with the two mysterious sisters alongside a coffin on a boat which is, he realizes, making for the cemetery. He calls her name, but she does not seem to hear him. He rushes to the police station, to report the incident, but the police are involved in the hunt for a murderer who has already claimed several victims. Although they are sympathetic to John's story, they hardly take it seriously. A couple of hours later he telephones England and finds Laura has arrived home safely. It is ironic that he thinks it is Laura who is in danger; we know already that he, too, may have second sight, and that he may be foreseeing his own funeral.

While Laura is away, John sees his daughter again: he chases through the back streets of Venice, over bridges and canals and through the swirling mist, into a deserted church where he thinks his daughter has taken refuge. He follows the little figure in the red coat, and calls and talks, hoping for a friendly response. At last, the 'child' turns round and there – instead of his beloved daughter – is a hideously deformed female dwarf, who produces a machete and hacks John to death. His blood flows along the floor of the church, and the following images transform the earlier messages as the film comes to its dramatic and gruesome conclusion.

Don't Look Now was filmed entirely on location in Venice and England, and in many ways it exceeds even Visconti's *Death in Venice* in its exploration of the city's atmosphere. Venice is the major moving force in both the du Maurier story, and in the Roeg film. An exciting psycho-thriller, it is full of visual and verbal shifts, about superstition and faith and the other-worldliness of religion. Repeated images, either juxtaposed or echoing more remotely, create surging associations. The opening sequences seem almost too calculated with their metronome precision of the red-stained glass, the red mackintosh, John throwing a packet of cigarettes, the little girl throwing her ball, the knocked-over glass and the spreading stain as John rushes out, too late to save his daughter.

When the bereaved couple reach Venice, red as a colour is associated not only with death, but with love and sex. The church is an ambivalent source of spiritual balance, and the spreading stain is like a forensic clue, linking with the Venetian police's frantic hunt for a maniac killer. (These sequences bring to mind a line of poetry from John Donne: 'I run to Death, and Death meets me as fast.') Many images run through the film, prefiguring danger, and music by the Italian composer Pino Donaggio complements these and the underlying sinister qualities found in Daphne's story.

Roeg's expertly conceived visual metaphors sustain a powerful foreboding. His Venice, like hers, is a grey workaday city of shadows and lapping water, its hotels emptying for the winter. Never has it been photographed so well, and the whole film is so atmospheric and pictorial that the acting need only have been competent. It was, however, excellent.

On its release, the film received stunning reviews: it was called an 'atmospheric, over complicated, but seriously frightening film', a 'stunning effective adaptation'. *The Spectator* declared:

'The best performance is given by Hilary Mason, as the blind psychic woman ... genteel and ordinary, until shaken like a leaf in a storm by her psychic powers. She inspires the right mixture of disbelief, graduating into fear and respect.'

Alexander Walker, writing in London's *Evening Standard*, summed it all up when he wrote, 'We'll be lucky if such a film experience is repeated.'

Daphne was pleased with it, too. On 14 October 1973 she wrote:

Dear Mr Roeg,

I must add my congratulations to the hundreds of letters and telephone calls you are surely receiving for the success of your film, 'Don't Look Now'. As you perhaps know, I was graciously given a private showing of the film when I was passing through London just over a week ago (I saw the US version!) and I was tremendously impressed by the whole thing, direction, camera-work, acting, story-adaptation. It is a strange feeling to sit and watch something one half-glimpsed some years ago in Torcello and Venice, later to write down on paper seeing, half dimly, through the character John's eyes, and then watch it transformed upon the screen.

I know I make the adaptor's work more difficult by too often writing a story as a narrator or through a single character's mind, which necessitates further invention on the part of the adaptor, and director, to enable a story and its people to come alive, and here you have succeeded admirably, indeed added more depth to unconscious thoughts that might have been my own!

Only once or twice was I puzzled, and this I think was in the motives of the priest (admirably acted) and his anxiety, and in one short superb scene where the two sisters were discovered laughing together. A red herring suggesting duplicity or merely healthy enjoyment?!

But no matter, it must have added to the audience's foreboding. And please, one of these days, find another of my short stories to screen!

Yours very sincerely
Daphne du Maurier

Seeing the US version rather than the British meant that Daphne missed the famous love scene between Donald Sutherland and Julie Christie, which was edited out so as not to upset American audiences. (Donald Sutherland told me, 'I enjoyed making the film immensely, although cinema audiences in the USA did not enjoy the picture that much.') At the time it was about as permissive as the contemporary cinema had ever offered. 'I still don't know what I missed, except from my son's graphic description,' Daphne said soon afterwards. 'The script-writers and director kept very well to the original, and what they put in helped to make the whole thing more convincing on the screen. All the reviews I have seen are very good, with the exception of the *Daily Telegraph*, but I don't see its readers turning out for an evening of suspense, from whatever quarter it might come!'

She was also impressed by the acting of Julie Christie and Hilary Mason, which she described as 'superb'. Julie Christie told me that she enjoyed playing the part of Laura, and liked her as a person. Her memories of making the film included staying in a rented house on the Guidecca in Venice, and of doing a lot of night shooting, to capture the empty feeling of Venice out of season. 'Nick Roeg spent a lot of time with the lighting to create the sinister atmosphere of the picture, and giving Venice this eerie feeling of dread and menace. I

Daphne standing by 'Yggy', her Polruan-built boat in which she and Tommy sailed on their honeymoon to Frenchman's Creek. This photograph was taken in 1965, the year of Tommy's death.

Kilmarth, the dower house to Menabilly, where Daphne spent the last twenty years of her life.

Nicolas Roeg directing Julie Christie in the 1973 film *Don't Look Now*. The film was to become a c̶
classic, and brought Daphne a new generation of readers. (*By courtesy of Nicolas Roeg*)

The atmospheric ending of *Don't Look Now*, in which Julie Christie leads the funeral party followed by Hilary Mason, who played the blind psychic, Heather. (*By courtesy of Julie Christie*)

Engrossed in a good book! Kilmarth, 1976.

In the front garden of Kilmarth in August 1978 my Aunt Bernice and myself – along with Ken and Mac – posed for a photograph with Daphne.

My last two photographs with Daphne: (*top*) inside Kilmarth in 1987 and (*left*) accompanying her on her morning walk along Par Beach in 1988. I was sad to see how frail she'd become. (*John Lyne*)

enjoyed working with Donald, and I think we did make a convincing married couple. That film, along with *Dr Zhivago*, is one of my favourites – though, looking back, I never thought it would become a cult classic. Every time anyone mentions *Don't Look Now*, they immediately have sinister visions, due mostly to Daphne du Maurier's chilling story.'

Don't Look Now was the first large-scale film for Hilary Mason, who won rave reviews for her portrayal of the psychic Heather. To generate more sinister tension, Roeg told her that the audience should be able to believe that Heather might be either good or bad. Her trance scenes were carefully directed; in the first, she recalled, he told her, 'You can make people believe you are trying to get Julie into your grasp when you tell her, "I can see your little girl."' The second trance was difficult to get right, and Roeg continued to film the scene again and again, until Julie Christie and Hilary Mason were nearly hysterical. 'You are pushing the spirit out of you, it's coming from the depths,' Roeg urged them. It was Hilary's own idea that, in the last trance, when she tried to warn about impending doom, she should have an epileptic fit, an idea the director accepted. 'Roeg is a totally exhilarating man to work for,' she said, 'and he manages to obtain startling performances from his actors.'

'We filmed *Don't Look Now* during January and February 1973 in Venice, which was very cold and empty. Nick gave Venice sinister qualities, and I remember Julie Christie saying how wonderful the light was, like the inside of a pearl. I had to wear two pairs of contact lenses (which was very uncomfortable) because Nick wanted to photograph me really closely. With these in, I could only just see. At the end of the film, in a scene where Heather was supposed to be guided by her sister, Nick said, "Leave her, let's see what she'll do," and I kicked my toe against the steps as if I really were blind.

'Nick was very kind to Julie, who was understandably nervous and worried; she told Nick, "You want me to walk and talk at the same time." Her hair had to be recurled for almost every shot, because the damp in the air made the curls drop out; Donald Sutherland wore a wig.

'His vertigo scene in the church was difficult to film. The stuntmen didn't want to do it, and Donald did quite a lot himself. Watch that scene very carefully, and you'll notice a pole – that's Nick Roeg pushing Donald further out! The dwarf who murders him was a flower seller from Rome. She didn't need much make-up, she was exactly as you saw her on the screen. While she was on location in Venice she was escorted around the city by two full-sized circus people who looked after her. She would never have managed on her own, but she was an enchanting person, with a lovely smile – I think she made some money from the film.'

During the 1970s *Don't Look Now* became a staple of programmes in film theatres all over the world, and surely it must be one of Roeg's most innovative films. He told me that the film did quite well in the States, and that it still plays to cinema club audiences all over the place. 'The calibre of writer Daphne was,' he said, 'is proved by the letter she wrote me ... Lesser writers would have objected to the changes that I made but somehow I had captured Daphne's initial vision, and she was pleased with my results.'

He has not yet attempted another du Maurier story, although Daphne felt that there were 'several awaiting a cunning hand'. 'Don't Look Now' is not only a tale of two civilizations, English and Venetian, but also a confrontation beween two kinds of mind, the rational and the superstitious. His adaptation of it just about finds a meeting point between psychological realism and Gothic fantasy; his treatment is such that the spectator is soon caught up in seeking the visual clues rather than finding the dramatic faults.

It is as landmarks in the development of the modern Gothic tale that film treatments of Daphne du Maurier's work stand out. *Rebecca* is a classic story of the 'other woman' with a twist. The continuity of time itself is in question in *Don't Look Now* as the future blends into the present. And in both that film and *The Birds*, forces arrayed against the protagonists leave their places in the accepted order, when lovable children and even harmless birds become evil, life-threatening creatures.

8

Kilmarth

Mine is the silence
And the quiet gloom
Of a clock ticking
In an empty room,
The scratch of a pen,
Ink-pot and paper,
And the patter of the rain.
Nothing but this as long as I am able,
Firelight – and a chair, and a table.

'The Writer', *The Rebecca Notebook*

Kilmarth, which in Cornish means 'retreat of Mark' is the ancient dower house to Menabilly, a fine old building overlooking the great sweep of Par Bay. It became the retreat of Daphne du Maurier in 1969 because the Rashleighs wished to move back into their ancestral home. Daphne was not at all pleased that she could not remain in the house she loved, and on which she had spent thousands of pounds repairing and maintaining; but Menabilly was Rashleigh property, to do with as they pleased.

The move greatly upset Daphne, who – according to those who knew her well at the time – was never the same person again after her world had been thus turned upside down. Though she appeared to forgive the Rashleighs, privately she continued to resent their occupation of territory she had made so intensely her own.

After Philip Rashleigh took up residence visitors were not encouraged. 'He doesn't like anything to do with the fact that I set several stories at Menabilly,' Daphne told me. 'I can't understand why. The place is so changed, they keep geese there now.'

He was annoyed by the number of people who came knocking on the door. 'Is this where Daphne du Maurier lives?' they would ask or, if they were better informed (and even more irritatingly), 'Is this where Daphne du Maurier used to live?' They were a constant reminder that his house had achieved a fame of its own, entirely outside his control, and due to the tenant he'd turned out. I visited Menabilly once while he lived there. 'Why do you want to photograph the house?' he asked me. 'It is a private dwelling now.'

After a while, Daphne would walk in the grounds of Menabilly once a week, on a Wednesday, but not before several months had passed: too much of her former life with her husband had been lived there. While he was still treasurer and comptroller to the Duke of Edinburgh, Tommy had begun to be troubled by ill-health, and he had retired to Menabilly in July 1959. The friendship with the royal family persisted, however. The Queen and the Duke of Edinburgh visited Fowey, and the Brownings received signed Christmas cards from the Queen and Prince Philip and from the Queen Mother. (The cards continued to come after

Tommy's death, but Daphne never kept them. She would give them to fans of the royal family, or simply to people who asked for them.)

Although Tommy had signed the lease for Kilmarth, he did not live long enough to make the move there. He had visited the house with her ('I like this place. I can see ourselves here,' he said), but he died on 14 March 1965. His last few years had been rather unhappy ones, not helped by reports in the local papers of his being charged with driving while drunk after a series of accidents on the Truro road.

He had indeed taken to drinking heavily and suffered from circulatory problems, particularly in one leg. This eventually developed into gangrene, though the doctor gave the cause of his death as 'sudden coronary thrombosis'. Daphne had engaged nurses to look after him at home at Menabilly, but it was still a shock to her when one morning 'he turned his face to me and died'. Her husband had been the handsomest man in his regiment, and always one of her heroes (though she recognized that his limited intelligence over some matters did not make him a completely competent soldier). They had been married for thirty-three years and now she was fifty-eight. Widowhood was very difficult to come to terms with.

His cremation was, as their wedding had been, private. There was no memorial service, but those who wished to do so were requested to send donations to the Security Fund for Airborne Forces. Browning was well known in the armed forces, but he was perhaps respected rather than liked. Major-General Frost, who under Browning had commanded the 2nd Parachute Regiment at Arnhem, remembered 'no jolly times in the officers' mess'. Talking about his former commanding officer and his wife, he said: 'Browning was a rather forbidding character, and did not enjoy socializing a lot. I never came across Daphne at any function, until after his death, when she came down to Aldershot for the naming of the Browning Barracks.'

Although he was stern and unbending towards his brother officers, Browning, like a great many soldiers, behaved very differently with his own family. He had sometimes dominated Daphne, and now his absence – 'not the separation of war that we had known twenty years earlier, but separation for all time' – caused her great pain. Everywhere were reminders of her loss: Tommy's Polruan-built boat, *Ygdrasil*, in which together they had sailed to their wedding so long ago, was outside on one of the lawns, used as a summer house. To ease her grief, she took over some of Tommy's things, wearing his shirts, sitting at his writing desk and using his pens to answer the letters of condolence that flooded in.

Unaccustomed to long hours spent alone, Daphne planned the changes she would make to Kilmarth with the help of an architect, a builder and his craftsmen. When, eventually, the move was completed in June 1969 she realized that she had been lucky to have had so much time to make the transition from one home to another. 'Day by day, week by week, month by month, I would visit the empty house, walk round the rooms, plan the decorations, decide where the furniture would ultimately go ... creating a renewed Kilmarth which I felt very certain its predecessors had loved.'

From the late 1960s until her death, she was looked after by Esther Rowe, who lived in the small cottage next door to Kilmarth and took care of everything domestic. Daphne enjoyed living in a large house, but anyone meeting her unawares might have been forgiven for thinking she was the local bag lady. Never one to spend a fortune on clothes, she dressed constantly in shabby slacks. From a distance, and particularly when she was wearing an old cap of her husband's, her small figure looked masculine rather than feminine. The inhabitants of Fowey and Par grew used to the eccentric, even unprepossessing, appearance of their local celebrity, and on occasion would tell enquiring visitors that Daphne lived elsewhere.

After Tommy's death her holidays were usually taken with her son Kits and his family, for she still enjoyed travel. The holidays influenced her writings: for instance one she had spent in the beautiful Italian hill town of Urbino before her husband died gave her the setting of Ruffano for *The Flight of the Falcon* which was published in 1965.

Daphne had learned to drive, though only automatic cars, and found Kilmarth a more accessible house than Menabilly had been. Not surprisingly, her admirers sometimes wandered down the drive and 'invaded'. This was not altogether a new experience: Daphne told me that during the 1950s people would often walk across the fields to Menabilly and 'peer in at the windows', hoping to catch a glimpse of her at work.

She was never rude, but while her husband was alive, they always gave anyone they saw walking along the coastal path at Pridmouth a wide berth. Tommy Dunn, the farmer from Menabilly Barton, commented: 'In many ways, Daphne and her husband regarded the Menabilly estate as their private principality, and intruders weren't really welcome. Although she never refused an autograph, I never heard of her going to a bookshop to sign books, either.'

Daphne suffered from a sense of insecurity which made her always a retiring person, who didn't enjoy the round of social gatherings and literary parties (on one occasion, before speaking at a literary function as she'd rashly agreed to do, she was actually sick). Much of this can be blamed on her father, Gerald, who had been possessive and sometimes 'difficult', but Daphne had loved and respected him beyond reason. He had indeed encouraged her somewhat erratic behaviour, and she often gave the impression that she was 'stuck up'. The common touch was never her forte, and her upper-class tendencies permeated the majority of her work. Humdrum lifestyles were not for her, and not good box-office either.

Kilmarth had ancient foundations, dating from the fourteenth century, and she found that this house, too, cast a spell over her. Items left behind by the previous tenant joined with what she had learned of the house's history to stir her imagination; images of the past crowded in, and she threw herself into her work.

'My predecessor at Kilmarth had been a professor of science,' she told me, 'and some of his things had been left behind. There were embryos in jars, and other intriguing things ...' These were the starting point for some of the short stories included in the volume entitled *Not After Midnight* (published in America as *Don't Look Now*), and were also part of the inspiration for *The House on the Strand*.

Written from a masculine point of view, it is a brilliant combination, part straight novel, part story of suspense. The descriptions are almost photographic and as we travel from page to page we see Cornwall in both the twentieth and fourteenth centuries. Dick Young, the central character, is staying in a house on the south coast of Cornwall where Professor Lane, a biophysicist, normally lives; he agrees to act as a guinea pig while he is there. Professor Lane has discovered a new drug, and the bottles are waiting for Dick in the laboratory at Kilmarth. The prescribed dose has the effect of a time-machine, carrying him back six hundred years into the same – yet different – Cornish landscape.

On successive days, Dick Young travels back in time, always returning to the same settings. Like an invisible man he witnesses intrigue and adultery, even murder, and somehow curiously feels himself personally involved. Hallucinations? Subconscious escape from his own life? Or has Dick really travelled back in time? This is Daphne at her most beguiling, in charge of a story that moves swiftly towards a startling climax.

'My most lasting memory of Daphne,' said Sheila Bush, her editor at Gollancz, 'is connected with *The House on the Strand*, a brilliantly constructed tale which is set partly in the present and partly in the fourteenth century. Daphne had an astonishing gift, which sprang, in part, from her narrative power. The action takes place in and around Kilmarth; I was somewhat confused about the topography, so I went to stay with her for a few days. Daphne dressed in the shabby but elegant trousers she habitually wore, and crammed an old cap of her husband's on her head. Through her eyes I saw a fourteenth-century otter hunt, and felt Dick's shock as he was carried back five hundred years, plunging across a twentieth-century railway line.'

The House on the Strand, with its combination of the historical and the psychic, was very well received, and the reviews ('a totally compelling story'; 'the du Maurier style grips you throughout') pleased Daphne. The only thing that disappointed her was that a film was never made of it. She had written it – she told me – almost as a film script, and it was her favourite of all her books.

It was in spring 1969 that Daphne was made a Dame Commander of the Order of the British Empire, but it was her daughter Tessa who went to Buckingham Palace to accept the award on her behalf. Daphne had refused to leave Cornwall to attend the ceremony in London.

Much as she loved her grandchildren, it was a disappointment to Daphne that she seemed to have failed to hand on the du Maurier talent she had received from Gerald and Kicky. She did go up to London from time to time to attend family weddings, for her children's children were growing up and marrying, but she grew increasingly solitary and eccentric throughout the 1970s, the period when I knew her. Now that she was a widow, there was little to coax her out of Cornwall and she much preferred to walk alone with her dogs down to the beach or along the coastal path. She was as fond as she had ever been of the Cornish countryside, its magic as beguiling to her as it had been thirty years earlier.

Esther Rowe was almost always there, and would protect her from over-zealous fans if they arrived at the back door. At the end of Daphne's life Esther would deal with her post, but during the 1970s Daphne did it herself. Letters came to her from all over the world, and Daphne wrote her replies on an old typewriter. Often she made mistakes, but this made her letters the more amusing. She enjoyed writing letters – for years she sent me approximately one a fortnight, and during the long, hot summer of 1976 she began one: 'Dear Daphne – I must be going mad ... I mean Dear Martyn!'

Her final novel was written at Kilmarth, and she began it with her usual skeleton of notes, roughing out the characters and the plot at first, then following this with six or seven months of writing each day from 10.30 until lunch at 1 pm, then resuming again from 6 to 7.30 pm. But it was a golden rule with her never to write on a Sunday.

Published in 1972, *Rule Britannia* was her thirteenth

novel, and she dedicated it to the actress Gladys Cooper –
they had known one another since Daphne's childhood, and
remained friends throughout their lives. She was a strong
character and, according to Michael Gough, 'When she
talked to you, she addressed the whole room with her
presence.'

Daphne told me that in 1970, the summer before she
died, Gladys rented a house not far from Kilmarth, and
brought along her younger daughter, Sally, and two
grand-daughters 'whom she quite clearly adored', Emma
and Justine. 'She'd come over for lunch – she had enormous
energy. On one occasion I offered to drive her down to the
beach, but Gladys refused and walked the two miles
unaided. She was then over eighty years old.'

Though she was exceptionally fond of her, Daphne herself
told me that Gladys was 'difficult, with a mind very much
her own, charging around the place with explosive energy',
and in many ways that is how she described the character of
Mad in *Rule Britannia*. Daphne hoped a film would
eventually be made of it, starring her friend. The dedication
reads: 'To Gladys, a promise.'

Years later, at a literary dinner in Birmingham, I was
talking to Gladys Cooper's son-in-law, Robert Morley, about
the novel and the prospects of a film being made of it. 'Yes, I
remember the dedication,' he said. 'It was a dreadful book,
not one of her best. It was a good thing that Gladys never did
make a film of it, thank God.'

Rule Britannia is set in a fictitious time after its political
leaders have withdrawn the United Kingdom from the
Common Market and, threatened with a nation on the verge
of bankruptcy, have decided that the solution and their
salvation lie in a union with the United States – something
they present to the people as a partnership, but which is seen

by the more perceptive as a takeover. A distinguished actress has retired to live in Cornwall with her grand-daughter, Emma, who has nicknamed her 'Mad'.

One morning they awaken to find their world shattered; the radio and phone aren't working, the post does not arrive, and they can see a warship at anchor in the bay, while American troops are advancing across the fields to their home. From the moment she sees them, Mad declares a kind of war on them; she is devoted to her home, and declares that she would certainly die for it 'if I thought it would do any good'. She rallies friends and neighbours to protect their heritage from these interlopers. Throughout the novel one gets the very strong feeling that Mad's sentiments are also those of the author, as she justifies her determination to defend their beloved Cornwall, helped by her grand-daughter.

Daphne had always been interested in the past, and she encouraged me to write about my forebears: 'It can be such fun,' she said. Apart from *Rebecca*, her most successful and best-loved novels are historical, but they had never received the recognition by critics which they deserved. She had always wanted her work to be taken more seriously, and perhaps it was a combination of these factors which led her to write biography again. *Golden Lads: Sir Francis Bacon, Anthony Bacon, and Their Friends*, was published in 1975, and it was followed a year later by *The Winding Stair: Francis Bacon, His Rise and Fall*. She was disappointed that neither *Golden Lads* nor *The Winding Stair* achieved much success, and she reflected sadly, 'The trouble is, I'm afraid, that the public sees me essentially as a novelist and not as a biographer.'

The research, however, had been interesting. Daphne

discovered that the Bacon brothers' maternal grandmother, Ann Fitzwilliam (a friend of Cardinal Wolsey) had been one of the first people to live at Milton, the house on which she had modelled Manderley in *Rebecca*, and in which she herself had stayed as a child.

It was also while she was engaged in this research that Daphne resumed her acquaintance with with her celebrated neighbour, the Cornish historian and writer Dr A L Rowse. They had known one another for at least thirty years, for the acknowledgements to *The King's General* thank him (with his name misspelt) for his 'great kindness in lending books and manuscripts'.

He visited Kilmarth for lunch, and Daphne listened as he talked and talked about Elizabethan history and legend. In return he invited her for lunch at his small, but charming, home on the coast near St Austell. His housekeeper remembers the visit: 'I went to the door, and there was this person dressed in an anorak and trousers, with small red Wellington boots, and an old fisherman's cap pulled down over her head. I wondered who on earth it was!'

In his book, *Friends and Contemporaries*, published shortly after her death, Rowse wrote what he described as 'the first serious study of her work'. 'I have done her proud,' he told me. ' "But beneath this delicate, beguiling exterior, I detect an element of masculine steel and stoic courage. She always wanted to be a boy, disliked being a girl and the business that goes with it. No less than five of her novels tell the story in the first person singular, as a male character." ' (These five novels are *I'll Never Be Young Again* (1932), *My Cousin Rachel* (1952), *The Scapegoat* (1957), *The Flight of the Falcon* (1965) and *The House on the Strand* (1969).)

Daphne, it is true, had a rather ambiguous air, especially when seen out walking, and she was indeed a strong character who feared no one. She was happy only in her own company, or in that of her family or close friends, people who knew how to respect her eccentricities, her privacy and her lifestyle. (I never wrote about her until she was eighty, despite her telling me that I was the only person fitted to do so.)

One such friend was Mary Fox, who had known Daphne from childhood, had been with her on the day they failed to discover Menabilly, and lived not far away from her. 'At least once a week we would meet for a walk with the dogs. This was usually down to Pridmouth Bay, when she lived at Menabilly, and then Par Beach after she'd moved to Kilmarth. Daphne would sometimes swim in the sea off this beach in the summer – she enjoyed that. I don't remember discussing her work a great deal, I think she liked to cut off and forget during her walks. Although she habitually wore trousers, she gave them tremendous style; I think she did have enormous style with her clothes.'

Before she became ill, Daphne's remarkable energy was evident all the time – despite her advancing age, she went out with her dogs at least a couple of times during the day. The fresh Cornish air, she believed, 'did her good'. A friend of mine meeting her for the first time described her as being 'like a little bird' – she was small and slightly built and still pretty. Never a large eater, during the late 1970s she began to lose weight. This prompted her to go for check-ups, but she was told there was nothing to worry about: 'the heart is fine'.

There were things to worry her, of course. In 1974 Cornelius Ryan published a book called *A Bridge Too Far*, and Richard Attenborough made a film of the same name which was released in 1977. Daphne raised no objections to the way her husband was treated in the book, but she took great exception to Attenborough's finished film. She told me, 'They were looking for a fall guy, I knew it would happen. My God! They wouldn't have dared do it if Tommy had still been alive. He would have taken a horsewhip to them and roasted them.'

Dirk Bogarde, who had served under Browning at Arnhem, played him in the film. He told many people how much he admired Browning, and it is rumoured that he wanted to play him with a little more sympathy than was portrayed in the final version.

A Bridge Too Far caused a sensation in Daphne's family circle. Despite her desire to avoid the limelight, she was so incensed by its treatment of her husband that she decided to have recourse to the courts to protect her husband's reputation. Eventually the case was settled out of court, but the whole incident had upset Daphne greatly.

Her daily routine varied little in her last years. She still rose at about 9 o'clock, rang her sister Angela at Ferryside, then had breakfast. She took her bath at about 10, and at half past she started to write and to answer any mail. Lunch, served by the dedicated Esther Rowe, was always 'simple food, without too much rich sauce' and always at 1pm. After lunch came a walk with the dogs, then perhaps a little more writing before settling down to the television with her 'sups'. 'People imagine me being waited on by a butler with a silver tray,' she said, 'but here I am, boiling an egg for my supper!' I'd rung just before *Rebecca* was about to be shown. 'I'm a great telly fan,' she told me. 'I know it's a conversation-killer, but I enjoy it.'

In 1977, to celebrate her seventieth birthday, ITV made a television programme about her, directed by her son, which included an interview with Cliff Michelmore. She appeared relaxed and content, but it must be confessed that she did say some rather odd things: how, for instance, she liked talking to sheep, and why she would rather be a shepherdess in the mountains of Crete. Friends thought she came over well, but Daphne reflected: 'I am glad it is all over. It was fun, but I did feel like a Gloria Swanson or someone. Anyway, I want to work on a new book in the autumn.'

In late 1978, soon after the visit to Kilmarth by Joan Fontaine which I mentioned in the opening chapter, Lord Olivier was on location in Cornwall making a horror film. He stayed at the Fowey Hotel. One very rainy evening, as the Cornish weather turned sour, he rang Daphne – to her surprise. 'It was funny,' she told me. 'First Joan Fontaine, then Laurence Olivier! He was charming, and invited me to have dinner and a drink with him at the hotel. It was such a dreadful evening that I declined the invitation – maybe I should have gone down to meet him.' Never very fond of mixing, she was gradually withdrawing further and further, though she did write to John Gielgud when he sent her a copy of his autobiography, *An Actor and his Time*, in 1979. 'I admired her enormously, although she was a retiring person,' he told me. 'That is why I was so thrilled when she wrote me, thanking me for my book, which she enjoyed reading.'

In March 1979 Daphne asked me to attend the American Film Institute's Life Achievement Award for Alfred Hitchcock on her behalf. 'What shall I say to the old boy?' she asked me. In the end, she composed a message which read: 'For Hitch, who was successful at filming some of my stories. Love, Daphne.' I was unable to take her message personally as she had requested; the tribute clashed with a television interview I was doing with Sophia Loren. I don't think that she even considered going herself.

One of the people whose company she might have been expected to take pleasure in was Tod, her former governess.

But Daphne refused to go and see her in her long retirement, because – it is rumoured – Miss Waddell had let it be known that she dispproved of aspects of Daphne's private life. And now, like all elderly people, she found that those she had known and loved the longest were dying – but not always of natural causes.

Lord Mountbatten had stayed with them, Tommy had been his chief of staff in the Far East, and his murder by the IRA in 1979 greatly distressed her. I happened to be in Cornwall at the time, and her feelings about his assassination were obvious to me.

There was a resurgence of interest in the work of Daphne du Maurier with three television productions in four years. BBC2 was the first to take the plunge, dramatizing *Rebecca*. Filmed in Cornish locations and starring Joanna David and Jeremy Brett, it was shown in four parts in January and February 1979. It was repeated the following year, being broadcast this time on BBC1. Caerhayes Castle was chosen to represent Manderley, something that Daphne did not entirely approve of. 'The Rashleighs have refused them the use of Menabilly,' she told me. 'Still, I do think Caerhayes Castle is too turrety, not a bit as I imagined Manderley to be.'

In 1979 I tried to interest her in the idea of writing a book about Cornwall, but her reaction was: 'That is just the sort of book that would upset my neighbours, the Rashleighs, and I do not want to be invaded by any more tourists. I get so many people calling to get books signed.' *The Rebecca Notebook*, published by Doubleday in 1980 and a year later in the UK, was mostly a collection of pieces written over the more than forty years since she began making notes for *Rebecca*.

After the success of *Rebecca*, there was a convincing BBC1 adaptation of *My Cousin Rachel* which closely followed the original; again it was in four parts and filmed in Cornwall, on the north coast. It was shown in March 1983, and Daphne commented: 'I thought Geraldine Chaplin miscast as Rachel. She was interesting, but hardly the person I'd imagined as my heroine.'

Independent television also got in on the act when Harlech TV serialized *Jamaica Inn* in a production which starred Jane Seymour, Trevor Eve and Patrick McGoohan. This was filmed in Cornwall and the West Country, and appeared on television screens in May 1983. 'I enjoyed filming Daphne's *Jamaica Inn*,' Jane Seymour recalled. 'We reconstructed the old inn and tried to film the story as she'd written it. I feel she is a very under-rated author, and I am pleased that she enjoyed my performance.'

One of the strengths of Daphne's writing had been to capture the essence of Cornish history and purpose, and she knew that many of her stories had been fed back into the folklore of the area. Never a charitable person at the best of times, although she was interested in the future of Cornwall Daphne was not prepared to make any financial investments for its future. She never got involved with local activities, and there is no du Maurier Village Hall; some locals grumbled that for one who had gained so much from a place she had given little back, but still she felt Cornwall was hers, and she would have no rivals.

At this stage she was still hoping to write another book, and I noticed how disparaging she had begun to be about other authors. She had little time for Lady Antonia Fraser, writing a funny letter to the magazine *Queen* about historical biographies which I gather upset her. She was also critical of Winston Graham: 'I can't understand his success,' she would say to me. 'All his Poldark stories are so predictable.'

We remained friends, and every time we met exchanged presents. She gave me many signed books, as well as photographs of her house and from her films, while I usually took her flowers. She was always willing to sign a book for me, or for a friend, but her memory was erratic. She once gave me some books, then at the end of my visit asked me, 'Where did you get those books from? You know I didn't give you them!'

It was in autumn 1981, after returning from a holiday in Scotland with her son, a holiday that she had hoped would provide her with information for a future novel, that she began to feel unwell. At first she was just tired, and told her friends, 'I will be better by spring.' But her health did not improve and her patience gave way, though she would put on a front when she met fans or friends, trying to delude herself that all was well and that she still could write another book.

She criticized everything, nothing was right and nothing was her fault – poor Esther Rowe bore the full brunt of this. 'She is living in the past all the time now. She throws tantrums, screams, shouts and stamps her feet. Sometimes I don't think I can control her,' she said despairingly to me one day.

A doctor diagnosed a minor nervous breakdown and suggested that Daphne should relax and concentrate on a hobby – she had none. Writing had always been her life. As Daphne grew more difficult, and took to racing round the narrow Cornish lanes in her small blue automatic car, her family became extremely concerned, partly for her safety (and that of others), and partly because they did not want the public to find out the extent of her illness.

Daphne spent a short period in hospital in Fowey and in

Exeter, and after her return home was given tranquillizing drugs. It seems that after she ceased to take these her memory had gone, and with that her ability to write. To tell a story one must be able to remember it. Slowly her mental condition improved, but everything was different for her. Though few of her fans ever realized it, her writing career was over. From a distance she appeared hardly to have changed but she took even less interest in her appearance. Close to, her face looked tired and pinched, even under the heavy cover of make-up she sometimes wore, and her eyes had a far-away look as if she didn't take in a great deal of what was going on. However, she continued to recognize me and to greet me with a 'hello, dear' up to the time of our last meeting six months before her death.

In order to amuse her, Esther would sometimes invite celebrities to visit Kilmarth: one who came was Val Doonican, who brought several books for her to sign. Another was Peter Skellern, who lived locally; he was asked to play the piano, and dutifully obliged. Daphne started to put on weight and gradually her health stabilized, but she would never write anything new again.

One of the last holidays she took was in the Scilly Isles; it was not a success. She was not bothered by the many people who stopped her, requesting an autograph – she disliked the hotel and the food which, she told me, was 'heavy, with rich sauces'.

My first writings about her were articles for publication in *Cornish Life* and *The Lady* to celebrate her eightieth birthday. It was at about the same time that, encouraged by Daphne, I started work on my first book, *Daphne du Maurier Country*. 'You know I've never wanted a book published about me in my lifetime, but why don't you write about Cornwall, saying I did this and that? I will give my consent to that.' She chose photographs for the book from her own collection, and when I told her that a launch party had been arranged at the Fowey Hotel she said that she might attend. She cried off at the last minute, but she did agree to a photo session on the beach at Par, and the photograph duly appeared in the *Western Morning News* with the headline 'Queen of Suspense at 80'.

The book aroused a lot of local interest, and BBC Radio Cornwall based a six-week radio series of half-hour programmes on it. The series was an enormous success, and was repeated twice within the following twelve months.

Shortly afterwards, the BBC television programme 'Daytime Live' approached me with the suggestion of making a series of fifteen-minute programmes, also based on *Daphne du Maurier Country*. They were eventually shown in two parts in the year before Daphne's death, and finally as a tribute to her after her death in 1989.

During the recce for the series I approached Mrs Rashleigh (Philip's widow), asking if she was prepared to allow Menabilly to be filmed for the first time in years. My discussion with Veronica Rashleigh took a curious turn when I asked her how she liked living at Menabilly, and mentioned the lyrical description in *Rebecca* of the birds singing outside the house of Manderley. When the Rashleighs took over Menabilly from Daphne, she told me, there was no birdsong at all – the bushes were full of feral cats, presumably descendants of the line of animals I had seen walking behind Daphne so many years ago.

Daphne was deteriorating fast; her health was failing, and her memory and ability to talk to any purpose had left her. On one of her more lucid days she had said to me, 'I've tried and tried to write more stories, but it's no good. I just can not.'

During the 1980s Daphne had a nurse in full-time attendance, as well as Esther Rowe who dealt with all the mail and decided who should be allowed to enter the house. She could go nowhere without one or other of them, and in many ways they helped to protect her and to save her the problems of coping with over-zealous fans. Over the years, nurses came and went, and they all found it difficult looking afer Daphne. Never an easy patient, she was sometimes very impatient with the staff, and many could not stand this. Introduced to someone she might say 'hullo', but if she did she would then stick the newspaper up in the air and pretend no one was there.

A neighbour who had experienced this treatment told me: 'It was hard to get people to sleep overnight with Lady Browning, she was so difficult. One night when I stayed with her she said about three sentences to me: "Put some logs on the fire", "Get my supper" and "Turn my bed down".' Small wonder this neighbour wasn't prepared to stay with Daphne again!

She became very difficult to see, and I had to make do with phone calls or brief visits of only a few minutes. Nevertheless, I stayed in touch with her. Even though we lived hundreds of miles from each other, I rang her often – we might only exchange a few words about our dogs or the weather in Cornwall. On the rare occasions when I was able to see her, she seemed in many ways a figure of pathos. She felt her age and the cold and wore layers of clothes: two or three jumpers and a waistcoat or a cardigan. Her hair was now snow white, and her features were gaunt and frail. Her faculties were in decline, and she knew it. 'What do you want to see me for now?' she asked. 'I am completely dotty.' But her strength remained, and her love for her dogs. Her last two were Ken and Mac who, like their predecessors, always accompanied her up the stairs to 'Bedfordshire'.

By now her public knew that there would be no more books, and so it was surprising when announcements appeared for a new book, to be published in 1989. Though posters and advertisements claimed that *Enchanted Cornwall* was 'by' Daphne, the text was based on interviews given to a writer named Piers Dudgeon, combined with extracts from her previously published works and illustrated with photographs by Nick Wright.

By April 1989 Daphne was no more than a walking imitation of herself, a shadow of the person who had thrilled the world with her brilliant books. On the day before her death, she was seen pottering around the grounds of Kilmarth. I spoke to Esther, who told me, 'She is very frail now.'

When the nurse went upstairs on the morning of 19 April she found that Daphne had died in her sleep. By her bed, as always, was the black and white photograph of Gertrude Lawrence inscribed 'To Daphne, all my love, Gertie' and from a wall nearby smiled Tommy, wearing his familiar jaunty beret. 'It wasn't unexpected,' said Esther, 'and the family were more or less prepared for it, but it took a while to sink in.'

Daphne had never lost her royal fans (who are reputed still to enjoy her books), and they had never forgotten her. When the Queen and the Queen Mother heard of her death, they each sent flowers to her son as a mark of respect. Her funeral was private, with a short service for members of her family held at Tregaminion church near Menabilly, even though she was an agnostic. After the service her body was cremated at Bodmin and her ashes taken to Kilmarth and buried somewhere in the grounds; the precise spot is known to only a handful of people.

Months after her death, I was able to visit her grave.

Someone in the town had insisted that Daphne's ghost had
been seen in the grounds of the house. So I lingered under
that benign sky, along the heath and among the
rhododendrons, looking across Par Bay, towards the Helford
River and Frenchman's Creek, and I wondered how anyone
could ever imagine unquiet slumbers for the sleeper in that
quiet earth.

A LOT OF
— = MILES APART   but note, nincompoop!

Works of Daphne du Maurier

Novels

The Loving Spirit (London, Heinemann and New York, Doubleday, 1931)

I'll Never be Young Again (London, Heinemann and New York, Doubleday, 1933)

The Progress of Julius (London, Heinemann and New York, Doubleday, 1933)

Jamaica Inn (London, Gollancz and New York, Doubleday, 1936)

Rebecca (London, Gollancz and New York, Doubleday, 1938)

Frenchman's Creek (London, Gollancz, 1941 and New York, Doubleday, 1942)

Hungry Hill (London, Heinemann and New York, Doubleday, 1943)

The King's General (London, Gollancz and New York, Doubleday, 1946)

The Parasites (London, Gollancz, 1949 and New York, Doubleday, 1950)

My Cousin Rachel (London, Gollancz, 1951 and New York, Doubleday, 1952)

Mary Anne (London, Gollancz and New York, Doubleday, 1954)

The Scapegoat (London, Gollancz and New York, Doubleday, 1957)

Castle Dor – with Arthur Quiller-Couch – (London, Dent and New York, Doubleday, 1962)

The Glass Blowers (London, Gollancz and New York, Doubleday, 1963)

The Flight of the Falcon (London, Gollancz and New York, Doubleday, 1965)

The House on the Strand (London, Gollancz and New York, Doubleday, 1969)

Rule Britannia (London, Gollancz, 1972 and New York, Doubleday, 1973)

Short Stories

Happy Christmas (New York, Doubleday, 1940; London, Todd, 1943)

Come Wind, Come Weather (London, Heinemann, 1940 and New York, Doubleday, 1941)

Nothing Hurts for Long *and* Escort (London, Todd, 1943)

Consider the Lilies (London, Todd, 1943)

Spring Picture (London, Todd, 1944)

Leading Lady (London, Vallancey Press, 1945)

London and Paris (London, Vallancey Press, 1945)

The Apple Tree: A Short Novel and Some Stories (London, Gollancz, 1952); as Kiss Me Again Stranger: A Collection of Eight Stories, Long and Short (New York, Doubleday, 1953)

Early Stories (London, Todd, 1954)

The Breaking Point: Eight Stories (London, Gollancz and New York, Doubleday, 1959)

The Treasury of du Maurier Short Stories (London, Gollancz, 1960)

Not After Midnight and Other Stories (London, Gollancz, 1971); as Don't Look Now (New York, Doubleday, 1971)

Echoes from the Macabre: Selected Stories (London, Gollancz, 1976, New York, Doubleday, 1977)

The Rendezvous and Other Stories (London, Gollancz, 1980)

Plays

Rebecca – adaptation of her own novel – (London, Gollancz, 1940, New York, Dramatists Play Service, 1943)

The Years Between (London, Gollancz, 1945, New York, Doubleday, 1946)

September Tide (London, Gollancz, 1949, New York, Doubleday, 1960)

Screenplay

Hungry Hill, with Terence Young and Francis Crowdry, 1947

Television Play

The Breakthrough, 1976

Other Titles

Gerald: A Portrait (London, Gollancz, 1934, New York, Doubleday, 1935)

The du Mauriers (London, Gollancz and New York, Doubleday, 1937)

The Infernal World of Branwell Brontë (London, Gollancz, 1960, and New York, Doubleday, 1961)

Vanishing Cornwall (London, Gollancz and New York, Doubleday, 1967)

Golden Lads: Sir Francis Bacon, Anthony Bacon and Their Friends (London, Gollancz and New York, Doubleday, 1975)

The Winding Stair: Sir Francis Bacon, His Rise and Fall (London, Gollancz, 1976, and New York, Doubleday, 1977)

Growing Pains: The Shaping of a Writer (London, Gollancz, 1977); as *Myself When Young* (New York, Doubleday, 1977)

The Rebecca Notebook and Other Memories (New York, Doubleday, 1980 and London, Gollancz, 1981)

Films made from du Maurier titles

Jamaica Inn, 1939
Rebecca, 1940
Frenchman's Creek, 1943
Hungry Hill, 1945
The King's General (never completed), 1946
The Years Between, 1947
My Cousin Rachel, 1953
The Birds, 1963
Don't Look Now, 1973